What Is "Life" And How To Live It

RABINDRANATH
SAHOO

INDIA · SINGAPORE · MALAYSIA

Copyright © Rabindranath Sahoo 2024
All Rights Reserved.

ISBN
Paperback 979-8-89498-331-8
Hardcase 979-8-89556-601-5

Dedication

*This book is dedicated to my wife Manju and children
Rinam, Pritam, and Aishwarya.*

Exordium
*"Life is not a problem to be solved,
but a reality to be experienced"*

— Soren Kierkegaard.

Contents

Acknowledgement

I thank my **wife** who all along appeared me as best critic and top support. My writing spree started in India continued in UK, ended in India, a long journey in deed. All throughout I was encouraged by my sons and daughter, daughters-in-law, son-in-law who are also worthy of the honour.

My heartfelt thank goes to science loving **Bipad Sir** who inspired me to write the book. In such a great occasion I cannot miss the opportunity to thank **Premananda Pradhan, my guide and Rakesh Mandal who** landed their expertise on computer work and allied matters related to the subject.

I owe my gratitude and sincere thanks to the **editor** and all the editing team members of **NOTION PRESS** who are the real architect of the birth of my first venture, "What is 'Life?' and how to live it."

Biography of the Writer

Born on 15th August 1957 in a small village of Chhotadaudpur, Bhograi Tehesil, Balasore district of Odisha, Dr. Rabindranath Sahoo grew up in a land that is culturally rich, educationally vibrant and spiritually profound. Bhograi, the extreme end block of Baleswar district in Odisha, is bordered by West-Bengal in the east, the Bay of Bengal coast in the south, Baliapal tehsil in the west and Jaleswar tehsil and town in the north. Here were born many luminaries, who have excelled in diverse walks of life, earning both national and international repute. Chhotadaudpur being a satellalite village under Bhograi Tehesil remained unseen and uncelebrated for long. The village is graced by its nearness to the birth place of Late Padma Shri Dr. Manoj Das, the acclaimed writer-philosopher and closeness to sacred Chandaneswar Shiva Temple where countless devotees seek Lord Shiva's grace. Dr Rabindra, is the second son among four, born to his father Late Gajendra Nath Sahoo and mother Late Allahadi Sahoo in a family shaped by the challenges of feudal heritage and trials of poverty. His father though got teachership during pre-Independent India, could not keep up the job for his ailing father. The family was pushed to poverty due to failing crops with minimum cultivable land. Nurtured in such an environment, he flourished with a deep sense of curiosity, reflection, and commitment that later shaped both his professional journey as a doctor and spiritual growth and his ultimate inner quest into life's profound meaning.

As far as he can recall, childhood was a time of distress marked by want and recurring illness. Around the age of ten or eleven he was gently persuaded to step onto stage as a lead performer of a newly formed village dance-drama. Poverty left no room for choice and the word of the village head carried weight he could not ignore. Yet, in that humble act, a silent door opened- guided not by ambition, but by the unseen hand of grace- offering both recognition and sustenance to once- forgotten hunger and village too found pride in his name. The medals and coins he received were never wasted- they became books and notebooks- the simple gifts that kept the flame of learning alive in his hands.

Time waits in the shadows until the inevitable walks into the light.

After school hours, his everyday activity was to move to other village (mode of communication by walking even if far away) along with the troupe to sing and dance whole night as a sacred duty to commit. Coming back in the next day morning even if tired of nightlong performance, he used to attend the class regularly as if dragged by an unseen force. Very impactful bitter day experience still glows on the slate of memory- when the drowsiness betrayed him in the mathematic class, and the sting of the shame became the lifelong reminder. He was humiliated before the class which was beyond one's imagination and cannot be expressed by words. After that incidence, of course the concerned teacher was sacked by committee but he took oath to concentrate on study. He left the acting spree in spite of tremendous pressure. Though he stood adorned with applause and world of music and art beckoned with its seductive grace, he did not yield to its charms. Encouragement and honour may elevate a man but they do not define his path. He chose instead the path of quiet discipline over the allure of fame. His performance was so lively that it left a deep imprint in the society for years to come. It so happened that even after a decade, he was invited to act in a Odiya film by a producer. He of course acted in the film in a short role. He gently turned down the request from the *CINE PHOTOGRAPHER of the film* to move to Mumbai who recognised his talent in acting and invited to Bollywood industry. Though he stepped into the film world, compelled by earlier instinct he consciously turned away from its embrace – choosing not to pursue the industry further lest the allure of fame draw his family into life of economic uncertainty and fragile dreams.

After his departure, the dream that once stirred in the hearts of villagers quietly collapsed. With no one to fill his place hope and vision began to fade- not lack of will but for want of a worthy substitute. In the year 1970 during the class 7 board examinations, he secured the fourth position among his peers – a quite testament to his early promise and disciplined mind. In spite of shattering poverty, he pressed on to the studies, holding fast to the fragile thread of hope. His parents were only stewards in that darkness bore the weight of survival with quiet strength. And though the path of learning called to him he often stepped into the fields and labour of daily life – helping his father in cultivation and other humble tasks not out of obligation but out of silent solidarity. At last, fortune smiled upon him. In the final class 11 BSE Examination of Odisha held in the year 1974, he rose to the top – securing the first position among the hundreds of students. That singular triumph not only marked the culmination of the years of quiet perseverance, but also earned him a place among the distinguished hundred across the state who were awarded the coveted National Scholarship that year. Of course, a boon in disguise.

Four years past of that scarry 1970's school trauma again he was burdened by troubles and haunted by trauma. Call it what you will- a trial of time, a divine test in the race of life or the karmic fruit ripened by fate- but it was the noose cast by his own elder brother, that tightened around his neck, marking a moment not merely of pain but of cosmic reckoning. His brother was then working in Kalahandi, a remote district of Odisha. Before the publication of Board result, Dr Sahoo, by then went there for a vocational tour after completing board exam. The news of standing first in his class filled him with quiet exultation and in that moment of triumph his inner yearning for learning deepened. His brother had a very different plan and the very result struck a blow to his brother's vision which he had long harboured. Yet, despite his academic triumph and the promise it held, his brother insisted to abandon further study and take up a job- pressing him to earn for family to get rid of poverty. Pressed hard by his brother they both went to meet Mr Sharma, the designated authority for his recruitment to the post of phone operator. He vividly remembers how the phone inspector, Mr Sharma alerted his brother for the foolish act. Confused and angered by the unfolding of the situation his brother sent him back home with a short-sighted promise of entry in to a reputed, DAV Autonomous college Titilagarh, Odisha. When intimation letter for college admission failed to arrive home nor any information from brother reached a painful truth surfaced- he discovered that the application form he had carefully filled out had never been submitted and with it the door to academic had silently closed.

Returning home he was met with hardship and gnawing agony of uncertainty. Determined to pursue his academic dreams he moved from pillar to post seeking entry into government college- yet the doors remained shut. Then, as if moved by the silent tears of an innocent soul struggling against fate, providence intervened.

Sindhu Devi, the esteemed principal of Fakir Mohan College in Balasore- named after the legendary writer and first architect of Odiya literature and ranked among the finest institutions of Odisha – chose compassion over convention. She overruled the rigid admission procedure and granted him a late entry turning despair to destiny. (He had failed to submit the entry form in due time, though he had very high scores in board result). In the ISC university examination of 1976, Dr. Sahoo passed with first division honours- a commendable achievement by any measure. Yet, despite his success he fell short of fulfilling the principal's cherished dream: to see him among the top ten college pass-outs in the state. It was a moment where pride and disappointment quietly coexisted each casting its own shadow on the path ahead. In time, he came to recognize the mistake of overdependence- placing too much trust in a friend with whom he had shared the journey of study, and at the final moment the friend betrayed him.

In 1976, he entered the MBBS course by clearing the newly introduced entrance examination by govt of Odisha. Over the next five years he emerged not as a diligent student but as a multi-talented admired figure in the campus. Honest and helpful by nature he earned admiration from peers, seniors and juniors all alike. A, **skilled volleyball player, he captained his class team to championship victory only in his second year of study. He was a winner in pole-vault event in annual championship Athletic** meet in two successive years. **Sometimes happiness is but a faint murmur echoing through forests and rivers present yet overlooked in the haste of life.** Goutam Bhai, (a senior athletic friend as he used call him fondly) suggested to run his candidature for college sports secretary post which he humbly denied. **His peers unanimously chose him class representative in his third year of study,** not just for his leadership quality but for the trust he inspired. With the background in dance drama in his early years **he was pulled to the stage** and captivated the audiences with his performance. **As a poet** his philosophical songs found its **place in the college magazine reflecting his depth of thought and artistic spirit**. A committed learner he completed the final university examination with first division in the year 1981 adding academic excellence to a vibrant legacy of talent and character.

At 24, in 1982, Dr. Rabindranath married a gentle, innocent girl from a wealthy family in Hatbadra- a village in Mayurbhanj district, Odisha, located near Uparbeda, the birth place of Honourable President of India, Droupadi Murmu. Her father a devout Worshipper of Goddess Durga, claimed to possess the supernatural powers – an assertion that echoed the sacred walls of grand temple he had built on his own residential land. The temple still revered as family's spiritual sanctuary, stood as a testament to his unwavering faith.

Whenever Dr. Sahoo visited his in-laws, he was subtly drawn into the aura of divine presence. His father-in-law with quiet conviction, would hint at the mystical presence Devi Maa, planting seeds of spiritual curiosity in young doctor's heart, who was once tuned to modern life of materialism. It was those moments between rituals, the stories and silent power of belief – that Dr. Sahoo's first step in to spiritual realm began. Not through doctrine but through experience. Not through books (though book helped in his progressive journey) but through the living faith of a man who saw the divine not as distant but as dwelling with in.

The first turning point in Dr. Sahoo's philosophical journey came as if destined. Nearly thirty years ago, he led a family tour to South India – seven members in all: his wife- Manju, two young kids-Rinam and Pritam, his mother-in-law- Jashoda Devi, his brother-in-law- Bhagban and his wife- Binu. Among the sacred stops was the revered Sri Aurobindo Ashram in Puducherry. Moved by the atmosphere, they spontaneously decided to visit Dr. Manoj Das, the celebrated writer-philosopher, who hailed from the same locality as Dr. Sahoo though the two had never met before.

Dr. Das welcomed them warmly and as they sat together for a formal tour experience. Dr Sahoo felt compelled to ask a question that had long haunted him- a *spark- that was ignited by his father-in-law.* The question was on different dimensions of life that has echoed through the corridors of human enquiry:" *Have you ever felt the divine power of Shrima- Sri Aurobindo?".* The question was bold, straight and almost unexpected from me. But, Dr. Das, serene and smiling, replied with quite wisdom: *Have you ever tasted a pinch of sugar? How does it taste? Sugar is sugar- no one can explain it. But one can experience it".* The journey ended with visit of other holy places in south India but the answer lingered. That moment planted a seed- a philosophy not of explanation but of experience. Echo that once stirred quietly within began to magnify in intensity- resonating louder with each passing years as if universe itself has chosen to amplify its inner calling.

The timeless truth- time and tide wait for none- unfolded in Dr. Sahoo's life as a steady current carrying him towards trials yet to come. In,1983, he was officially posted to Jaleswarpur CHC as a Family welfare officer. Yet under political pressure he was abruptly deputed to new, Chandaneswar SHC in Chandaneswr- a remote underserved corner of Odisha where his true struggle began and, in many ways, still continues. The region is impoverished in every material sense, yet rich in spiritual essence (lord Shiva being the worshiped Deity)- the divinity of the land seemed to mingle with its very soil. As the lone qualified physician at the time, Dr

Sahoo bore the weight of daily hardship, social responsibility, and financial strain. The path of service was steep, and the burdens layered- enough to choke any hope of escape. But he stayed not out of obligation but out of conviction and worked and worked. His only strength lay in his unwavering honesty and truthfulness.

Dr. Sahoo's growing reputation- earned through his pivotal role in regularizing the Chandaneswar Sub-Health Centre from private controll to Government oversight, and his election as President of Chandaneswar Mahavidyalaya, Sahabajipur(close to West Bengal Border) did not sit well with certain politically aligned groups. Out of sheer jealousy, he was abruptly transferred to Manatri Govt Hospitalin Mayurbhanj a move widely regarded as "punishment posting"

The transfer was undesired, but not unfamiliar- struggle had become a recurring theme. At times he felt as though luck was mocking him. Manatri was remote, not suitable for schooling of the children, burdened and isolating. Yet for two years he endured serving with determination. Due to illness of his wife, he remained on leave. Eventually he was transferred to another near-by SHC offering a brief grimmer of relief. But fate had other plans. Just three months into new the new posting he made a difficult decision: to resign from govt service and devote himself fully to private practice. The decision to resign from government service was not born of personal choice alone- it was result of persistent political meddling. The then health minister, who hails from same locality was notably unsupportive of Dr. Sahoo's posting and under her influence environment grew increasingly hostile. With dignity intact but spirit worn thin he chose to step away-not in defeat but in protest against a system that no longer allowed him to serve freely.

Over the course of ten years and eleven months, Dr. Sahoo firmly established himself as one of the finest physicians in the region- respected by the good and sought after by the suffering. He founded a Nursing home in his residence in ground floor where the earning and serving ran in parallel, each reinforcing the other. **As his reputation soared, old adversaries – once silenced by his rise – reawakened, driven by political and personal envy. Their hostility escalated from mental harassment to threats of physical harm.** It became increasingly clear that the organised threat he faced was not merely a social or personal conflict- it bore a signature of darker force. Orchestrated by the wealthy man of the locality (the king-pin of gang of five), the act carried the weight of malice and manipulation echoing what mystics often describe as the workings of devil's hand. In spiritual traditions such targeted attacks are seen not just as human cruelty but manifestation of deeper, unseen battles between light and shadow.

In the midst of this storm, a divine intervention arrived in human form. Mr. Paresh Chandra Nayak, then Secretary to Chief Minister Shri Naveen Patanaik, suggested that Dr. Sahoo consider rejoining government service for second time. At that critical crossroads torn between uncertainty and conviction, he surrendered the decision to God. Perhaps it was the divine will – or the culmination of an unseen test of faith. But Mr Nayak stood by his side like an unmoving rock- an embodiment of selfless service and love.

He re-entered the service with renewed purpose in 2003, after a gap of 10 year and eleven months. His inner calling was unmistakable- quiet but resolute. It was not ambition, nor persuasion but a deeper voice within that guided him towards the decision. He holds an unwavering conviction that it was the whisper of God within- a quiet sacred guidance – that gently steered him through the storm of distress. Over the years (again sixteen years) earned three more promotions ultimately retiring from the post of Additional Director of Health Services Odisha on 31st August 2019.

Following his retirement, Dr Sahoo was invited to rejoin government service in post- retirement capacity by a highly placed administrative officer who held him in great esteem. Yet with humility and clarity he declined- choosing instead a quieter path of reflection and inner growth. Today, he finds joy and fulfilment in immersing himself in a wide spectrum of literature – from philosophy and spiritualism to autobiographies and teachings of mystics and seers. His reading list is a sacred tapestry woven with the wisdom *of BHAGVAT GITA*, Manduka Upanisad, Mahavatar Babaji, Lahiri Mahasaya, Swami M. Ram, Paramahamsa Yogananda (Autobiography of a Yogi, 1946), Swami Vivekananda, Ramkrishna Paramhansa, Bhagvan Ramana Maharshi, Radhanath Swami, Jiddu Krishnamurti, Srila Prabhu pada, Eckhart Tolle (Author of famous book, The Power Of Now, 1997), Shri M, Sadguru's Inner Engineering and many more. Each page offers not just knowledge, but a deep resonance with eternal truths that guided his life.

Spiritually his path has stretched from sacred heights of Badrinath to the southern tip of Kanyakumari-a pilgrimage across India's spiritual spine. The only exception are Darka, the ancient kingdom of Lord Krishna in Gujrat and Kamakhya temple at Hilltop of Guwahati, Assam which he still hopes to visit someday.

Alongside his deep study of philosophy and spiritual literatures, Dr. Sahoo continues to serve patients with unwavering sincerity at his own clinic. His commitment to healing and lending support to the sufferings remain as steady as ever- rooted in compassion and discipline.

He also finds joy in travel, often journeying to United Kingdom, where he has explored nearly all major historical and modern tourist destinations across England, Scotland, Wales, Northern Ireland. In his travel, Dr. Sahoo found joy not only in the breathtaking landscapes- the silent majesty of mountains, the whispering forests, the rhythmic embrace of the pristine beaches but also the silent contemplation they inspired.

Each journey became more than destination. As he wandered through mountain valleys blanketed with gazing sheep, a childhood memory stirred gently with in him-the simple rhyme of Baa Baa Black Sheep....; What once was a playful tune now echoed with deeper meaning. It reminds him that life in all its vastness, remains beautifully simple, quietly innocent, and deeply in tune with nature.

Standing at the edge of Wales, where the land surrender to sea, Dr. Sahoo gazed out from the extreme costal end point-his eyes stretching towards the far north pole, where man have reached to explore the nature and geopolitical ambition, an enduring act of quest to conquer the unknown. The horizon felt infinite, the air crisp with silence. In that moment the vastness of nature whispered to the soul, reminding him how small we are, and yet how deeply connected to the cosmos.

Beyond nature's grandeur, Dr. Sahoo also immersed himself in the marvels of human creativity. At Madame Tussauds, he witnessed the life like artistry that captures the fame and memory making alive; at British Museum, he walked through centuries of civilization, feeling the pulse of history in every artifact; and at the tower of London, he witnessed the power, intrigue, and resilience etched into its stone walls. In these man-made wonders, he observed how life flows – not just through people, but through legacy, imagination, and the silent stories that endure.

Amidst the beauty, he explored what life meant to others and more profoundly what it meant to himself. Enjoyment and inquiry walked hand in hand, as nature became both a sanctuary and a teacher.

Dr. Sahoo's life story began in solemn depth, yet it unfolds towards a conclusion shaped by divine justice and metaphysical truths that defy human reasoning. In the realm of mysticism and spiritual philosophy, there exists a profound teaching: ***never ever harm the innocent***, for God resides in their purity. This principle resonates across the traditions- from philosophies to Upanishadic reverence for the Atman in all beings, to Christian call to "become like little children" to enter the kingdom of heaven. Now even reflected in modern legal system because from ancient scriptures to modern constitution there is a shared belief that **harming the innocent is a grave moral wrong.** Mystics and Enlightened being have long taught that the acts of cruelty-especially toward the pure hearted do not vanish into silence. Instead, as divine law of moral balance, such actions rebound upon the perpetrator, often with grave consequence. ***The core idea is often called the Law of Divine Reciprocity or Specific application of Karma:*** that harming innocent creates a severe karmic debt that must be balanced, often in this life. Throughout history, the lives of sages, saint, mystics- from Ramkrishna Paramahamsa to Bhagvan Ramana Maharshi to Saint Francis of Assisi- have illustrated this truth. Those who harmed them often faced spiritual of existential crisis and consequences while those who honoured their innocence were uplifted. Many contemporary teachers frame it in terms of energy. An, innocent being, especially a child or saintly person has a pure high vibrational energy field. To violently attack that purity creates a severe energetic dissonance. The perpetrator's own energy field must compensate for this violent act often leading to crash in their own health, luck or mental stability.

The Law of divine reciprocity revealed itself as a living truth in Dr. Sahoo's life in many instances in the past and now an observed fact. The 'gang of five' driven by cruelty, attempted to inflict physical injury and deep mental harm upon him, the universe responded in its own silent justice. One by one (four of them) they met their end in a series of extraordinary events that seemed to echo higher cosmic judgement. The kingpin- the architect of malice – lives in a state of ruin and mental agony. A teacher recently deceived him in a land purchase deal and got punished with death his wife and shattered family life. Instances are many more beyond description of the book.

His spiritual journey as he says *'begins now'* and firmly believes that *'it will continue'*. After surviving spinal shock, Dr. Sahoo's life long intuitive force grew sharper- no longer a quiet guide, but a vivid signal. Within the soul of Dr. Sahoo intuition has never been a learned skill- it is an ancient whisper, a sacred pulse that rises unbidden like a tide beneath still waters. Often mistaken for mere emotion, his anger is not a reaction but a revelation-a storm that brews in the otherwise calm sea of his being when unseen begins to stir. It is the divine's way of speaking through him not in words but in waves.

One such moment opened out on his return from Badrinath in May 2024. The journey meant to be sacred, was pierced by discord. A sudden argument with family members triggered a surge of unrest- not of Ego rather against the self-Ego of a member- an output of intuitive alarm. Like a Storm rising from silence, he felt compelled to abandon his back seat and move to the front. Moment later, the front car wheel cracked ominously on a downhill slope. He asked driver to stop and the disaster was averted. That, shift born of no rational calculation, became a shield. The divine had spoken through the storm.

Yet not all warnings are heeded. The deaf boy, nephew of a humble shopkeeper beside Dr. Sahoo's clinic was the soul he cherished. Each morning, he would beckon the boy to visit him and open the medicine shop, to maintain the rhythm of presence and care. It was not routine for him by the time but a ritual of internal connection. But on 5th day morning, the 4th of June 2024, the boy did not come. He had chosen instead to engage in a dangerous electric work. That day he died- suddenly, silently, tragically beyond the reach of sound or plea.

In these moments and other so many instances, Dr. Sahoo saw the divine not in miracles but in the fragile threads of intuition and consequences. His anger is never fury – it is prophecy. His advice is never instruction – it is protection. And his life, woven with such threads, stands as a testament to the metaphysical truth that soul knows what mind cannot grasp. The storm within is not the chaos- it is the divine wind, warning, guiding, and grieving.

Word 1371.

Total 4185 words

Author's Note to the Revised Edition

In this re-edition, a new chapter "Ethics and Ethical Being" has been added to reflect the moral and spiritual dimension of human existence in the modern age of science and technology. The revised edition preserves the spirit of the original work while refining its form and depth in some chapters. The preface, introduction, biographical notes have been carefully fine-tuned for greater clarity, smoother flow and expanded vision.

Let these pages be quite mirror-reflecting not just words but the stirrings of your own thought.

Rabindranath Sahoo.

Preface

From a childhood of hunger, marked by economic fragility and daily uncertainty, I walked with struggle as my companion and courage as my guide, until at last I stood in the sacred calling of a doctor with depth and emotion. Hardship marked my path yet it could not deter my resolve to live a life of service. There was no empty space not even in dreams- only the dense weave of karmic consequence, pressing me into form. And from that compression the seed of dharma stirred. ***"What is life and how to live it"***- is the question that has echoed through the chambers of mind for long years not as a philosophical pastime but as a burning inner enquiry. It, reverberates with the awe of millions who have pierced the surface of existence and ask if there is more than science can ever explain. This question did not come to me in comfort but in harsh poverty of my early years to the modest stability I now inhabit. **Life revealed itself as both a test and a teacher**. Each encounter with suffering, resilience and fleeting joy unfolded as if existence itself were whispering my ear.

As a doctor my training taught me to trust science to seek answers in Anatomy, Physiology, pharmacology and neuroscience so on. Yet life is not confined to the dry vessel of medical science; it overflows into the unseen stream of intuition, spirit and mystery, where meaning truly resides. Real life defies the boundaries of biology. In moments of presonal struggles as well as extreme difficulty when reason faltered and suffering deepened to lowest level, I found myself leaning not on training or social influences but on intuition and right work (Bhagavat Gita). I discovered something extraordinary, a mystical strength a quite knowing and divine presence that seem to guide, protect and uplift those who walks the path of goodness even against impossible odds.

Throughout my profession I have stood close to the very threshold where life and death meet- the measurable meets miraculous. Over forty years of clinical practice, I have witnessed the mystery that defy the textbook logic. I have seen patient on the brink of death return to life with little care, as if sustained by some unseen force, while others slipped away despite the best that medical science could offer.

One moment remains etched in memory, even after twenty-five years. A middle-aged patient was undergoing major abdominal surgery in our operation theatre led by eminent Retired professor Dr. G. C. Poothal from SCB medical college Odisha. Everything began smoothly. But mid-way through procedure I entered OT to check on the progress- only to face the crisis. The patient was turning cyanosed. Professor Poothal looked at me and said **"Rabi, do something. The patient is slipping away"**. Thunder struck in my mind. With no time to deliberate I administered the lifesaving drugs with utter faith that the patient must survive. The prayer was heard. The patient recovered fully with completed procedure. He went home without any further complication.

And yet, life remains unpredictable. On 28th of August 2025, Dr Gradlin Roy- A 39 -year- old, young and accomplished cardiac surgeon from Chennai, (India) tragically passed away after suffering from a massive cardiac arrest. He was perusing his morning routine ward round and was having no known heart disease. He Collapsed Surrounded by Colleagues and Staffs. His final hour account- Dr.

Gradlin Roy quietly withdrew into stillness, his breath fading like a tide retreating from shore. Those near him felt an air of heavy with strangeness. The instruments of human control- machines, medicines, human touch- seemed powerless. His pulse faltered not like a falling heart but like a candle surrendering to a breeze no one could see. *The irony was heart breaking: a healer of hearts lost to the very organ he had devoted his life to saving.*

It is not merely a question, but an eternal abstraction- one that has stirred the minds of scientists, philosophers, mystics, seers across all ages. Life forms a living bridge between science, philosophy, and spiritual insight, inviting us into the eternal realm where only the most attuned feelers may sense the pulse of existence. It encompasses a universe of complexity far beyond the grasp of ordinary mind. The universe unfathomable to the ordinary mind reveals its mystery alike- to mystics, philosophers, poets and scientists, each touching the truth from a different shore. And if universe is a mystery to the awakened, life within it is an even deeper enigma-more intricate, more elusive, and forever. From primordial soup to the spark of human consciousness, life carries a memory older than time. It pulses through the veins of a hummingbird and whispers through the intuition of a healer. It is not merely what we treat- it is what we must honor. ***Life is not merely within the divine; life is the divine itself unfolding through time and form.***

In every heartbeat, in every breath, I have seen life not just as biology- but a sacred unfolding. My journey has not been to conquer life, but to understand it; Not to define it but to listen to it. To live a life is not merely to exist but to act with purpose, without attachment to outcome. It is to serve with sincerity, guided by intuition and anchored in duty. As Bhagavad Gita teaches, true living is a karma yoga- the path of selfless action, where work becomes worship and the soul finds peace not in results but in righteous effort.

In my own journey, I have found that life open out most meaningfully when we listen inwardly, act outwardly and surrender quietly to the divine rhythm that moves through all things.

"Life is the sacred choreography of consciousness through time- an unfolding spiral where we are called not merely to survive, but to awaken, dissolve craving and co-create with the infinite through love, clarity, and karmic responsibility".

word-989

Introduction

What is life not merely a question but a pilgrimage- from silence of the cosmos to the pulse of human flesh. Life is not static noun- it is a verb in motion, a spiral of becoming. It begins not with breath but with vibration. Before atoms, before stars and galaxies, there was rhythm- the heartbeat of all existence. From that primordial pulse, the cosmos unfolded -space, time, energy and the silent architecture of possibility.

Life a vessel on float

Life in its immediate sense begins with human body- the physical vessel through which the existence first makes itself known. The anatomy of flesh and bones and organs orchestrated by hidden rhythm of physiology forms the stage on which our days are enacted. Every heartbeat is biology in motion yet also the silent signature of being itself. Every breath is a prayer received from cosmos and returned to it. Amid the rhythm of heartbeat, the whisper of breath, and the endless tide of cellular renewal, there rests the ineffable mystery of what makes us alive. The human body is fragile yet indispensable stands as the vessel that sustain the drama of existence amid the vast uncertainties of being. As sailors must know their ship to cross the sea, so we must know the body to journey through existence.

If consciousness is the bridge

Physical process alone cannot account for subjective experience like Qualia-the inner world of awareness, meaning and purpose. This hard problem of consciousness is where the metaphysical enquiry begins. Unsolved problem- still haunts us -Is consciousness a mere by-product of neurons or reflection of deeper universal reality. Thomas Nagel's through his work "What is it like to be a bat?", argues that subjective experiences – what it's like to be a conscious being- cannot be captured by objective science. Science has failed to prove the consciousness being emergent property of brain. So the argument leans in later favor, then the physical life is not opposed to divine nature but participate in it like a wave arising from ocean.

Human Action, Responsibility and Ethics are the scaffolding of a cosmic architecture

The body is not just a vessel but a participant in thought. Maurice Merleau-Ponty argued that the perception and actions are intertwined in our bodily experiences of the world. In the crucible of actions and responsibility biology becomes choice and physiology takes form as behaviors. A human being is not only a living organism but a moral agent capable of compassion, cruelty, creativity as well as self-reflection. Our actions caries consequences far beyond our bodies, society and civilization.

Human life is not only a story of survival and growth but also story of choices. **We understand that life lived as biology risks being mechanical and bare instinctive**. Every action we take- whether small gestures or great decision- ripples beyond ourselves touching the lives of others and shaping the moral fabrics of the society. It has biological and evolutionary root, philosophical grounding and spiritual dimension. Ethics emerges as compass by which these actions are guided. **Right action, at right moment, in right way with the right spirit-anchored in wisdom, compassion, and surrender is the path that transform responsibility into sacred duty, and ethics into living truth.**

Death, Dying as threshold and Immortality at far end

Death is the inevitable cessation of bodily function and sharpens our question. Science describes death as collapse of system, but it cannot fully explain what if anything survives the collapse. Even in modern times the definition of death has been shifted to new length. **Death is not negation of life but it is the transition to another dimension of being.** Plato called the body the "Prison of the Soul" while Vedantic thought speaks of atman continuing beyond the perishable frame. Across the traditions and cultures and in spirituality and mysticism death seen as counterpart to physical not an end; a dimension where, consciousness, soul or essence may continue beyond the limits of mortality. Whether conceived as immortality, rebirth, or dissolution into a greater cosmic order this spiritual horizon remains central to the human quest for meaning.

In this book journey begins with body expands through actions and responsibility and moves into the mysteries of death and immortality where science, philosophy and spirituality meet at the threshold of existence. I have chosen a modest volume to reflect on essence of life; still the deeper question of how to live it shall be unfolded in chapters to come.

It is not a manual – it is the mirror. It reflects readers own voyage, from-stardust to soul, from instinct to insight. It does not preach but it whispers.

Word-771

Chapter 1

Science at a Glance

Definition of Science

Science is a term originally came from the Latin word Scientia which meant knowledge, a knowing expertness or experience. By the late fourteenth century, Science meant in English collective knowledge.

We are not going details of whole development of science and technology but the general concept of science at a glance.

A) Science is defined as "The systemic study of the natural world and it's physical and biological processes through observation, identification, description, experimental investigation and theoretical explanation." Reference 1 http://www.oxfordremference.com

The systematic study of the structure and behavior of the physical and natural world through observation, experimentation, and the testing of theories against the evidence obtained and technology is the application of this knowledge for practical purposes.

B) Science is the pursuit and application of knowledge and understanding of the natural and social world following a systematic methodology based on evidence. (Reference-2)

In nutshell applying established physical and natural laws gathering knowledge out of experimentation making new theories upon which further development takes place. So, it is a "KHOJ" in physical and natural world appealing to ours five sense organs and the mind as well as intellect.

Question arises is there anything beyond this?

It is true that science has tremendous gift to the society in the form of modern days all gadgets, from driverless car to airships and rockets, from humanoid robots to experimentation of development of deathless human form (GODHOOD). It has developed technique to explore the deep sea, the inside of the earth, extra-terrestrial objects, and the universe at large and designed medical equipment and medicines to cure the disease and establish pleasure taking out pain and suffering of the patient. Even man is thinking to create an artificial earth (digital earth at least) to maintain the sustainability of human life. In brief science-philosophy has tried to narrow down the gap between the physical reality and imaginary wish of the humanity.

But can this life be sustainable in the lap of complete dynamism of science and technology?

- What is the first atomic bomb story about? Was it created for everlasting peace of the society or destruction of the society, a show of self defence or self-Ego? Was it created out of curiosity of pure science?

- Answer to all the questions is simple. In world war 1, there was a chaos produced out of self-Ego akin to war of Mahabharata between Kauravas and Pandavas in Kurukshetra. There was disturbance in equilibrium in universal consciousness. Resultant effect is destruction. (Creation and destruction is the rule as envisioned in Hindu mythology.

- To gather some of the ideas on science and spirilism let us go down in the memory lane to explore some of the quotes of eminent personalities of the world.

Erwin Schrodinger an Austrian physicist (12-08-1887 to 04-01-1961), winner of Nobel prize for physics in 1933 who made significant contribution to quantum mechanics was profoundly influenced by eastern philosophy including Bhagavat Gita. In his book, "My view of the world" Schrodinger wrote, "One of my key interests was the concept of unity of all existence". The idea that individual self (Atma) is connected to the ultimate reality (Brahma) is reflected in science of quantum mechanics. Advaita Vedanta philosophy, the concept of non duality aligned with his scientific view on the nature of reality in quantum mechanics. He admitted and quoted in another time, "Most of my ideas and theories were heavily influenced by Vedanta.

Warner Heisenberg a German theoretical Physicist (05-12-1901 to 01-02-1976) born in Wurzburg, Germany, begged the Nobel prize in physics in 1932. He was influenced by eastern philosophy and found parallel between core philosophy of Bhagavat Gita and interconnectedness of quantum mechanics. During his visit to India in 1929 he met great philosopher Rabindranath Tagore and publicly said, "Anyone who read these ancient texts will not find quantum physics amusing; rather, it will help them understand the intricacy of quantum mechanics much better."

J. Robert Oppenheimer, the father of the atomic bomb was born on April 22 1904 in Manhattan, New York and passed away on Feb 18th 1967 in Princeton, New Jerscy. He was present during the first bomb explosion, "Trinity" test on July 16th 1945 in new Mexico Desert. After witnessing the explosion he recalled a famous verse from Bhagavat Gita, "I am become death, the destroyer of worlds". (Reference-3) He learned Sanskrit in 1933 and read the Bhagavat Gita in original form citing it as the most influential book to shape his philosophy of life. He listed T. S. Eliot's, "The Waste Lands", the book itself inspired by Upanishads, as the other influential book in his life.

Albert Einstein born on 14th March 1879, in ULM in the kingdom of Wurttemberg in the German Empire and passed away on 18th April 1955, in the Princeton, New Jerscy. On 14th July 1930 Rabindranath Tagore visited Albert Einstein's house in Caputh near Berlin. The conversation between them on how to understand truth and reality was recorded and subsequently published in January 1931 issue of modern review. There is no documented record of discussion on specific topic of Bhagavat Gita between them but both Tagore and Einstein admired the text. There are few quotes by Einstein –

i.   "The Bhagavat Gita is the most profound philosophical song ever written"

ii.   "The more I study science the more I believe in GOD."

iii. "There are only two ways to live your life. One is as though nothing is a miracle. The other is as though everything is a miracle".

iv.   "On August 6th 1945 first atom bomb dropped on Hiroshima Japan. "Woe is me" Albert Einstein upon hearing the news of Hiroshima bombing.

Now it is evident that great other scientists are also influenced by eastern philosophy and religious scriptures of various religions of the world.

Though not documented anywhere, Einstein, the blessed child of God, could think in line of new theory influenced by Hindu philosophy to strengthen the postulation behind creation.

Thus, in my opinion, great Einstein who is the pioneer or E=mc2 may have taken the leaf from our Hindu scripture (Veda & Gita & other scriptures)

E = The supreme energy or the absolute energy: (The energy released out of atomic fission in physics term)

M = The mass, the human body: (Materials in terms of physics)

C = Consciousness, the spiritual power in human body: (Speed of light, another form of energy in physics) I will not be wrong to interpret Einstein theory of E=mc2 in light of spiritualism.

We can attain the enlightenment equivalent to E, the supreme energy, the GOD, when our consciousness will be multiplied near infinity to merge with him.

In another incidence

Scientific analysis on material nature of physical world is depicted as GOD's phenomenon in Hindu scriptures. Let us find about it.

On June 18, we 2004 a remarkable statue of Lord Shiva was unveiled at CERN (The European Centre for research in particle physics) in Geneva. This statue depicted Shiva Nataraj, The Lord of dance and stood two meters tall. Fascinating connection between cosmic dance of Shiva (ultimate Yogi in Hindu scriptures) and behavior of sub atomic particles in quantum mechanics has captivated both physicist and spiritual thinker alike. In 1972, Fritjof Capra published an article titled "The dance of Shiva: The Hindu view of matter in the light of modern Physics". In this article he opined the parallels between Shiva's dance and behaviors of subordinate particles. In the dance of sub ordinate particles mirrors Shiva's cosmic dance where creations and destructions are fundamental aspect of existence.

The co relation between the science, philosophy and spiritualism is exhibited in the book SPRITUAL SCIENCE by Steve Taylor (An American Singer, Song writer, Record producer, Film maker & actor). Here he has drawn pan spiritist view that explores various puzzling aspect of science and world drawing insights from physicist, philosopher, mystics, and spiritual traditions. In the book He suggest that the reality is more then what we perceive physically. He believes that consciousness as the fundamental reality.

One quote from professor Freeman Dyson (Theoretical Physicist Princeton Institute for advanced study) worth mentioning. It states, "I do not make any clear distinction between mind and God. God is what mind becomes when it has passed beyond the scale of our comprehension. God may be world-soul or a collection of world-soul. So, I am thinking that atoms and humans and God may have minds that differ in degree but not in kind".

So where lies the life, which is manifested phenomenally all over the universe? What is relative and absolute truth? Is science and spiritualism being contradictory to each other or science is a sub version of spiritualism? According to eminent scientist Professor D.H.R. Barton (born on September 8,1918, Gravesend, Kent, England-died March 16,1998, College Station, Texas, U.S.) Nobel Prize winner for chemistry TEXAS A & M University, "God is truth. There is no incompatibility between science and religion. Both are seeking the same truth."

So in one eye science is "what we see and believe" but in spiritualism on the other, we first believe then see through our inner eye.

Chapter 2

Physical World and the "Life"

Preface: Millions of scientific activities are under taken around the globe to know and establish "what is life". Efforts are being made to keep life alive on world or elsewhere in the universe at any cost out of fear for natural/catastrophic mass extinction. It is yet far from truth. Life as a whole is the truth known to spiritual and religious community (believers) from time immemorial.

life evolution in context to the universe, a scientific look:

In my previous discussion, I did deal with "the science at a glance". I initiated with definition of science and technology and its social affects along with little spiritual thought related to it. Now let me discuss about the universe, the creations and the phenomena attached to it.

What is universe?

Scientific

Nasa defines universe as "The universe is everything. It includes all of space and all the matter and energy that space contains. It even includes time itself and, of course, it includes you. Earth and the moon are part of the universe, as are the other planets and their many dozens of moons."

In essence the universe encompasses everything from tiniest particle to grand cosmic structures that stretches across the unimaginable distance. Reference-4—Science.nasa.gov

"The universe is literally everything, the sum of all existence" Reference-5_Lifescience.com

Creation of the Universe

I) Big-bang Theory

So many theories are proposed to find out the exact cause of creation of universe, the first step of creation of physical world, but unanimity is clearly lacking. Out of all the Big Bang theory is most accepted one. Georges Lematre, the father of big bang theory was a Belgian catholic priest, theoretical physicist, mathematician, astronomer, professor of physics at catholic university of Louvain. In 1927 he proposed the theory based on observation and theoretical consideration. It was influenced by Einstein's theory of relativity.

According to the theory, around 13.7 billion years ago entire universe was condensed in a infinitesimally small, primeval' super atom of infinite denseness and heat called singularity. Cataclysmic explosion of this singularity leads to sudden expansion causing ballooning out at a speed greater than the speed of light. This effect caused cooling down as a result, mater and energy were formed. The afterglow effect of big bang is cosmic microwave background radiation (CMBR) which was formed 380,000 years after big bang, discovered in 1965. Hubbles law on observation of galaxies moving away from us provided additional support. By nucleosynthesis after few minutes of big bang light elements like hydrogen, helium, trace amount of lithium was formed. Cosmic evolution is the final phase, occurring billions of years after big bang when galaxies, stars, planets, were formed due to gravitational interaction.

II) Inflationary universe Theory

This theory explains the flatness of universe which is reality, not fully understood in big bang theory. It is said to be due to rapid expansion in an exponential rate, smoothing out the irregularities, causing flatness of universe.

CMBR has the same temperature, about 1 part per 100,000 in all directions, not explained in big bang is proposed in this model of inflationary theory. It is said that the region that once were contact reached thermal equilibrium during this phase.

There still problem with all theories, which haunts scientific community -the problem of something out of nothing. How the Singularity came in to existence at the first place.

Other theories are Steady fast theory, cyclic model, slow freeze theory, plasma universe theory String theory and multiverse hypothesis, Black mirage, Theory of eternal inflation, Quantum fluctuations, conscious universe, Hindu cosmology. Conscious universe model being philosophical Hindu cosmology being more mythological.

III) Conscious universe Theory

Though not a single individual is credited for this theory, some eminent personalities are=

Galileo Galilei—Over 400 years ago Galileo recognized certain qualities like colours, smell, taste exist only in consciousness. He felt that if living creature were removed these qualities will vanish.

Greek thinkers like Aristotle and Thales hinted at pan-pchism. They proposed that all things posses some form of mind. Italian philosopher, Francesco Patrizi in 16th century coined the word 'panpsychism'

John Wheeler a physicist proposed in 1950 that there was no universe till the consciousness arose to perceive it. He denied that reality is physical, and there is deep rooted connection between consciousness and existence.

British physicist, mathematician, and philosopher, ROGER PENROSE, who won noble prize in 2020 in physics, introduced a key element of panpsychism by advocating that consciousness is rooted in the statistical rules of quantum physics especially in the microscopic spaces between the various neurones of brain. Penrose has contributed to the book 'consciousness and universe: quantum physics, evolution, Brain and mind' which delves with the connection between consciousness and universe from perspective of quantum physics. (Ref -goodread.com)

This theory is basically new thought on concept of consciousness. Principle of consciousness is no more seen as the emergent property of brains of advanced organism.

Panpsychism suggest that consciousness exists throughout the fabrics of universe, and is the fundamental aspect of reality akin to mass and electrical charges.

Cosmo psychism attribute the most fundamental aspect of consciousness to the cosmos rather than the physical ultimate.

Cosmo psychism takes panpsychism further. It proposes that the consciousness of the innate and ordinary individuals are derivatives of it. From it's view point the universe is seen as living, sentient, and whole with consciousness pervading everything. This inherent mind was present since the birth of cosmos.

It bears enormous importance when seen from Hindu philosophy. Cosmo psychism resonates with the Hindu concept of consciousness as both individual inner principle (Atma, Jiv atma), and universal (Paramtma), the eternal, and all pervading. In Bhagbat Gita chapter 13 verse 23 Lord Krishna explains the relation between Atma (individual soul) and paramatma (supreme soul). Herein we may conclude that science is not at contradiction with spiritual/religious thought laid down in Hindu philosophy, hundred thousand years ago.

ATMA

- Atma (Jivattma) = It is the individual soul, the conscious spark residing within each living being, identical to paramatma but not equal to it.

- It is identified with body and mind, experiencer of thought and emotion and actions but distint from physical body and mind.

- The atma is subject to the laws of karma and undergoes cycle of birth and death.

- Atma, being eternal and distinct from physical body possesses free will. It has capacity to make choices and decision.

PARAMATMA

- It is the eternal, all pervading, unchanging reality, the supreme soul or universal soul or GOD.

- it is present everywhere and every living being, including man and govern the cosmic order.

- Paramatma is imperceptible to the senses but resides with in the etheric heart of all living being.

- It is the overseer and permitter of all actions that Atma undertake but not directly interfering the actions.

- It is the support, that sustain atma

- It is the enjoyer that witness the play of creation

- It transcends all material existence and is purely spiritual.

- Paramatma accompanies the atma through different life time noting actions and bestowing result based on karma.

Analogical representation of Atma and Paramatma is like two birds sitting on the same tree (physical body) where one bird (Atma) is eating the fruits of the tree while other bird (Paramatma) is simply watching with out eating.

N:B The more details will come up during spiritual context.

IV) Hindu cosmology of creation of universe

There are lot many beautiful stories in different religions of world on creation of world. Hindu belief system is the outcome of old Vedic principle and stories.

Hindu cosmology of creation of universe:

Mythological and scriptural descriptions of creation of universe in various religions of world are plenty and diverse. In Hindu philosophy also the creation of universe is mentioned in Rigveda, the oldest of all scriptures (written), composition is dated roughly 1500 to 1000 BCE. The text has been orally transmitted since 2nd millennium BCE. Hindu puranas that also describe the origin of universe include several texts each offering a unique philosophical perspective on cosmology and creation of universe. Notable among them are, Brahmanda purana -based on concept of cosmic Egg Bhagabat purana -describing the process of creation is an act VISHNU through the creator god BRAHMA, and Vishnu purana - which describe the creation by VISHNU through transformation of primal substance, (energy) Prakriti in to various elements and forms of life. Early puranas were composed between 350 CE to 750 CE and later puranas between 750 CE to 1000 CE.

NASADIYA SUKTA, in Rigveda commonly known as Hymn of creation is a cosmic song denotes cosmogony, elaborating the state of universe on the Eve and during creation of universe. It starts with 129th shloka (followed by 6 more shloka) of 10th mandala of Rigveda.

THE English translation of 1st shloka as,

> "Neither Existent nor Non-Existent was there, neither matter nor space around. What covered it, where it was and Who protected? Why that plasma, all pervading deep and profound"

The above state of neither existence nor- non-existence is science paradox. That itself is the truth which is beyond comprehension of human brain. No space means no dimension. Matter was not created by then.

2nd shloka as

There was neither death nor immortality nor was there the torch of night and day,

The one breathed windlessly and self- sustaining, there was that one then, and there was no other

This hymn here is elaborated in yogic sense. Prana, in yogic term encompasses breath, life force vitality, energy. Therefore pranayama refers to conscious management of breathing. So state of 'breathlessly breathing' is that to impress upon a flow of energy within not revealing as a life form. No light mean, if light is taken as matter in science term, no matter was creatd by then. If taken in term of revolving universe, (day and night) it may be postulated that the state was static.

Issue of death, or immortality comes after existence of a state of physical form.

In 3rd sloka

At first there was darkness wrapped in darkness, uninterrupted continuum of cosmic water

That one which came to be, enclosed in nothing, arose at last, born of power of heat.

The very first statement 'darkness wrapped in darkness' qualify the original state of neither existence nor non-existence.

Secondly out of heat the, boundless, ever pervading, cosmic plasma born.

The 4th sloka

In the beginning desire descended on it that was primal seed, born of mind.

The sages who have searched their hearts with wisdom

Know that which is kin to that which is not.

Again here it refers to the primary state as 'cosmic mind' from which the desire or 1ˢᵗ impulse Generated heat, and the subsequent, cosmic water.

The sages had wisdom due to purity of their heart, could know the link between 'that is' and 'that is not'

In 5th Sloka

And they have stretched their cord across the void,

And know what was above and what below

Seminal powers made fertile mighty forces,

Below was strength over it was impulse.

The consciousness, of the sages was powerful enough to transgress the void and know the reality of the state of creation that happened with impulse, above crest, below as the creative energy.

In 6ᵗʰ Sloka

Who really knows, who can declare? When it started and where from and where will creation end.

This statement again refers to early state of 'neither existence nor non-existence', which is known to creator only non less than HIM.

7ᵀᴴ Sloka

That one, out of which creation came, may hold the reigns or not perceiving all

From above, that one alone knows, the beginning may not know too.

Here is the opinion of management of existence 'the reign in the hand of created energy' or the supreme force as pervading, is uncertain.

The universe thus created may or may not know the truth of creation. Even gods do not know as they came after creation.

Creation of the Universe in light of Spiritualism

"Cosmic-ego-trip" theory by Andrew may published in 16th July 2021 states "the law of physics involves a handful of fundamental constants that determines the strength of gravity, electromagnetism and subatomic forces. As far we know these numbers could have any possible values if they departed even slightly from the value they actually have, the universe could be different place, most importantly for us "life" as we know it -including of course ourselves – could not exist. Some people see this as evidence that the universe was CONSCIOUSLY designed for human like life to evolve – the so called self-centered anthropic theory proposed by Nick Bostrom in his book- 'Anthropic-Bias'."

If the creation of the universe is a conscious process, there is possibility of conscious creator of infiniteness "THE GOD". Other questions which haunt the science community if something can be created out of nothing. when the universe, matters, dark matter, energy, dark energy, is a proved possibility the source may be infinite "THE GOD" beyond the comprehension of human mind.

Creation of "Life"

When atoms learned to dream, life began- and the universe awoke within its own creation

Before molecules danced and cells remembered, there was silence- pregnant with possibility.

Life did not begin with certainty, but with a question:

Can matter dream? Can chaos compose rhythm?

From cosmic dust to hydrothermal whispers,

From RNA's fragile ambition to panspermia's wandering seed, each theory is a myth of emergence-a mirror held to the mystery we call being

To ask how life began is to ask how meaning awakens.

Through the study of natural abiogenesis, the idea is put forth that life arouse from non-life more than 3.7 billion years ago. Study of evolution reveals the means of biological transformation from simple life form till most complex structural life form (Human) found in nature. As far theory postulates our mother, earth is 4.6 billion years old. Human roamed on earth only 3 to 7 million years ago. Modern human with big cerebrum refined intelligence originated in Africa in past 2 lakh years only. So, the evolution of universe precedes the evolution of life.

Life on earth is thought to have begun through a process called Abiogenesis- that is, non-living chemical compounds gradually organizing to self-replicating, metabolizing systems. The simple organic molecules- built from water, carbo dioxide, hydrogen and other basic ingredients- under favorable energy and environmental gradients- self organized into complex polymers capable of replication, metabolism and evolution. Laboratory evidence supports that **RNA-like molecules**, lipid membranes and catalytic networks can spontaneously emerge under prebiotic conditions **forming protocells** that bridge the chemistry and biology. Though the precise pathway remains unsolved, the growing consensus implies that life is not an exception but an outcome of universal laws of complexity- a natural ascent of matter towards self-awareness.

These early protocells evolved over millions of years, developing genetic codes, metabolism and membranes, until a singular lineage emerged that gave rise to all known life: LUCA, the short form for Last Universal Common Ancestor LUCA was not the first form of life, but the last common ancestor from which the domains of Bacteria, Archaea, and Eukarya descended. It is not a single cell preserved in time, but a hypothetical ancestral population that lived around3.5 to 4.3 billion years ago. It's considered the biological root of the tree of life and studying LUCA helps scientists understand how life emerged from non-life in earth's early condition.

After LUCA, lineages split into simpler single-cell life(prokaryotes) and then eventually, into eukaryotes-cells with nucleus, organelles, and more complexity. This allowed multicellular life, new body plans, and eventually the animals, plants and fungi.

Yet the ultimate truth still eludes definition: even as science deciphers how life began, the question of why consciousness arose from matter remains the most profound mystery of existence.

While science speaks of LUCA as the first common ancestor of all life, spiritual and philosophical traditions have long intuited a similar truth in symbolic form. In Hindu thought, it echoes the emergence of life from Brahman, the undivided reality that differentiate into countless beings-**"Ekam sat, vipra bahudha vadanti**", *the one truth, seen as many.* In spiritual tradition this echoes the idea of non-duality, where all forms are expression of one underlying reality.

Tat Tvam Asi-Thou art That

LUCA represents the beginning of biological continuity, the flow of life, a thread unbroken through billions of year. Philosophically, this mirrors the samsara cycle of birth, death and rebirth- where life is a flowing river, not a fixed point.

Though LUCA was not conscious , it carried the potential for consciousness. This parallels mystical traditions where divine essence lies dormant in matter , waiting to awaken.

LUCA is like the seed of Brahman-silent, formless, yet holding infinite possibility.

In ancient mysticism, this primal source is described as cosmic seed, the first awakening of consciousness from the stillness of void. Greek philosophers imagined a **Living Cosmos (Anima Mundi),** while Taoist sages saw it as a spontaneous arising of forms from the formless Tao. Thus, LUCA becomes not only biological ancestor but a metaphor for unity behind diversity- the eternal life principle expressing itself through infinite forms. To the mind of science, LUCA is a cell; to the heart of philosophy, it is the first remembrance of **Being**- where the universe began to know itself. LUCA emerged from prebiotic chaos-how? Science offer hypothesis, but mystery remains. This invites philosophical awe, akin to cosmic wonder, where the origin of life becomes a sacred question, not just a scientific one.

If LUCA is revealed in truth, the veil over life's origin will lift- and in that moment, science, spirituality and philosophy will converge into a single stream of knowing, where the question of being finds its root.

Thus, the birth of life is not merely a biological event but a cosmic awakening- where universe through living forms, first

looked upon itself and whispered, *I am*

Panspermia hypothesis- This hypothesis proposes that life did not originate on earth. Life may have originated from primitive biological material- such as microbial spores or organic compounds- carried by extraterrestrial bodies like comets or asteroids or interstellar dust, rather than arising independently on earth.

This concept suggest that the building blocks of life or even viable microorganisms could survive the harsh condition of space and seed life on a hospitable planet. It changes the earth centric view of biogenesis and opens the door to a cosmic perspective on life's origin.

The RNA, World Hypothesis proposes that life on earth began with self- replicating RNA molecules that both stored genetic information and catalyzed chemical reactions- function now divided between DNA and proteins. This theory elegantly solves the "chicken-and-egg" problem of which came first: genes or enzymes since RNA can act as both. Scientists have synthesized ribosomes-RNA molecules that catalyze reactions, including their own replication. RNA world offers a testable, mechanistic bridge between chemistry and biology.

Definition of "Life"

"Life" is defined as,

1. "An organismic state characterized by capacity for metabolism, growth, reaction to stimuli and reproduction" Ref.- 6 (Merriam Webster)

2. "it is a self-sustaining chemical system capable of Darwinian Evolution" Ref.-7 (NASA)

3. "Condition that distinguishes animals and plants from inorganic matter including the capacity for growth, reproduction, functional activity and continual change preceding death, the origin of life" Ref.-8 (OXFORD LANGUAGE).

So definition of life has been numerous depending upon the characteristics of living being (Reproduction, metabolism, evolution, energy, autopsies etc.) but we have yet to distinguished between the "life" and living matter where life lives. Though scientific community have different opinions on definition of life, unanimous conclusion to is yet to reach. From such definitions common human mind is drawn towards a clear-cut dividing line between Biologic and a biologic form of objects. Human life is most precious, integrated with physiology, psychology, sociology and law enforcement needs better discussion.

So far during discussion we have some ideas on 'Life' in general. Here I would like to discuss a few definitions of 'human Life' in scientific and philosophical way keeping spiritual and religious definitions as separate entity (2nd volume). I hope it will be clear the relationship between science, philosophy and spirituality eventually.

What is human Life? How to describe it? The aim of Life? What is its purpose? How to make a Life journey? Where does this human civilization heading? Should it be meant for fulfilment of body desires? Does it begin within mother's womb and ends with the death of the individual? When birth and death happen to human Life? Thousands of complexities and contradiction and mysteries both seen and unseen comes out when we try to dissect out the human Life in any way (spiritual, religious, philosophical and scientific). Sir Isaac Newton discovered the fundamental laws of nature (law of gravity). His magnificent work "Philosophiae Naturalis Principia, Mathematica" (Mathematical Principle of Natural Philosophy) in 1687 was breakthrough in Scientific knowledge on natural law of universal gravitational force. His remarks worth noticing in philosophy of life.

"I see I have made myself a slave to philosophy."
(Reference-9)

"I do not know what I may appear to the world but to myself I seem to have been only like a boy playing on the sea- shore, and diverting myself in now and ocean of truth lay all undiscovered before me" (Reference – 10).

If these are the views of the great scientist ever born on his discovery and on philosophy of life and work, the definition of 'human Life' still a bigger philosophy yet debated.

To acquire some knowledge of "what is life", "human life" in particular, we need to understand what is meant by "human", we are not beasts; though there are some bestiality instincts within us. Animals are driven by instincts and the need to survive only. of course, recent studies prove that some categories of animals have higher intelligence. Off and on, we also witness such human-like activities through electronic media posting and literature, still the difference is distinct and apparent. We are not God either. If religious scriptures, spiritualism, and philosophies are to be believed. Human beings are mortals with limitations and flaws, rather than divine beings.

Human life is the harmonious expression of matter, mind and consciousness- a continuum where biological evolution meets the self-awareness.

Scientifically it is the highest form of organised energy, sustained by cellular intelligence and coded memory of DNA, evolved through billions of years of natural selection. But in our opinion life cannot be defined solely by science, for science though can explain *how* it evolved, remains silent on *why* it did so. Science deciphers the patterns of universe-the expansion of space, the emergence of life, the architecture of consciousness- yet cannot reveal why the existence chose to be. The equations of biology describe the process, but not the purpose. The spark that turned inert matter into living consciousness still escapes the microscope. Perhaps the life is not merely biological phenomenon but a **cosmic intent**- an unfolding of awareness through form, a dialogue between the finite and infinite. The ultimate intent is veiled by mystery for- human mind is bound by the very reality it seeks to transcend.

Philosophically, it is the mirror of existence- a being capable of questioning its own origin, meaning and destiny. Philosophy seeks meaning, but every answer opens another question, not able to answer the final *why*.

Spiritually, human life is the manifest breath of the divine, where consciousness awakens within form to experience truth, beauty, and compassion. It whispers that existence itself is the intent-that the universe is not the product of purpose but the unfolding of awareness seeking to know itself through infinite forms. Perhaps cosmic will is not external but **immanent**, breathing through every atom and heartbeat, expressing itself as evolution, thought and compassion. Still the final truth- what stands behind being, behind purpose and behind time itself remains beyond comprehension. Our intellect reaches only the shore of the infinite ocean, sensing that behind all forms and motion lies the silent purposive order- the unknowable ground of being. It is the silence before creation, the nameless reality from which all meanings arise and to which all return.

Until the mind rises beyond itself, the truth behind creation and existence will remain hidden- like light unseen because we stand with in its glow.

Thus, to be human is to embody the universe's long journey from atom to awareness from creation to contemplation. Ultimately, we may say, the human being is what human is- a unique synthesis of matter, mind and meaning. He has defined himself by his power and intelligence. He has proved his ability to utilize the natural laws of the universe, to manage the physical and the natural world for his own good. Science and philosophy, art, music, culture, traditions, laws, and ethics, as well as war, crime, and destruction, are all the by-products of living. Human life is affected by such occurrences and activities. Individual spiritual experiences, different religious principles (old and new), and philosophical thoughts have influenced human life since the time of human civilization.

The flow of Human Life: Science, Religion, and Philosophy

Human life is the confluence of three great streams- **Science, religion and philosophy** each presenting the different face of same truth. **Science** describes the body as the **evolutionary masterpiece,** shaped by time and environment, where atom becomes cells and cells become consciousness. **Religion** gives this consciousness a direction- it teaches that life is not accidental but intentional, a sacred trust linking the human to divine. Hinduism calls it Atman, Christianity names it soul, Islam speaks of Ruh and Buddhism calls it Awakening- each a reminder that beyond biological pulse lies the breath of spirit. Religion reveals the spiritual evolution of soul. **Philosophy,** standing between science and faith, searches for coherence- asking why awareness arises in matter and how meaning emerges from existence. Thus, human life must be seen as continuum- science in **form,** philosophy in **enquiry**, and spiritual in **essence.** To live as human is to unite all these dimensions to know through science, to question through philosophy, and to feel through spirit- until knowledge and wisdom and faith merges into one luminous understanding of being.

Common understanding of life and its meaning

Life as a journey or Test

Many people see life as a path of growth, filled with challenges meant to shape character. Across the cultures and continents, many people do find personal growth through religious and spiritual pathways. These mediums offer not just belief system, but frameworks for transformation, rituals of renewal, and mirrors for self-understanding. The evolving global religious landscape as documented by Pew Research, reflects not only demographic shifts but also humanity's enduring pursuit of personal growth, meaning, and spiritual development through faith based and transcended pathway

According to a Pew research Centre study 2012, approximately 84% of the world's population is affiliated with specific religion or belief system; 16 % are atheist or agnostic not religious and in 2020 found that- about 24.2 percent of world population did not identify with any religion. Again, latest breakdown from pew Research Center's June 9, 2025 updates (estimates refers to the year 2020, which is the newest globally comparable baseline in their dataset) shows major religious share Christians at 28.8%, Muslim 25.6%, Religiously unaffiliated(nones) 24.2%, Hindu14.9%, Buddhists 4.1% Jews~.2%, and all others including folk, Sikh, Jain, Bahai, Daoist at 2.2%.

Across the world's diverse language, traditions, faiths and philosophies, humanity seeks the meaning of life through different yet converging path. For many, **religion** offers meaning through devotion, moral order, and promise of transcendence- a sense that life has a divine purpose. In Abrahamic traditions (Christianity, Islam, and Judaism) life is often viewed as a test of faith and morality, with eternal consequences. In Hinduism and Buddhism, life is a cycle(samsara)- a chance to evolve spiritually and dissolves ignorance or the craving. Recent global studies by the Pew Research Center reveal that majority of people across the world still turn to religion, scriptures and scriptural teachings to find meaning in life. Despite advance in science and secular thought, faith continues to provide moral direction, emotional comfort, and sense of pure purpose that pure reason cannot satisfy. In many societies- from Asia and Africa to the Americas- the sacred texts, prayers, and rituals remain central to how people understand their existence, face suffering and seek hope beyond morality. This enduring reliance on religion signifies that human beings are not merely rational seekers of knowledge, but spiritual seeker of meaning. The world may evolve technologically, yet the heart still bends towards the timeless wisdom of faith-towards the belief that behind creation lies the compassion, and behind existence, divine intent.

Life as Relationship and Contribution

Across the cultures, people find meaning in Family, Love, and community. Selfless love is the primal thread of human essence- an invisible force that elevates the mortal to the superhuman. It is not coded in machines, nor replicated in algorithms. It binds the world not through logic, but through grace. In its presence, existence finds meaning; without it, even stars lose their song.

In modern times love life often sways between the pursuit of material gain and fading echo of a heart once attuned to the divine. Modern-day love often find itself in a paradoxical space-hyper-visible yet emotionally elusive, shaped by technology, shifting values and rapid cultural changes. When compared to legendary romances like Laila-Majnun, Radha-Krishna, Tristan-Isolde or Cleopatra-and Antony, todays love stories tend to emphasize individual freedom, emotional negotiation, and psychological compatibility over sacrifice, destiny or transcendence.

Yet yearning remains. Even in dating apps and digital flings, people still seek that **Majnun-like madness**, that Radha- like devotion, that epic sense of being chosen.

Contribution enriches the life's essence. Whether viewed through the lens of divine principle or human ethics, contribution is often seen as a sacred act- one that transforms existence from mere survival to meaningful participation. In many spiritual traditions, contribution is a form of **Seva (selfless service)** seen as a path to transcend ego and align the divine will. The act of giving- whether through compassion, creativity, or care- is considered a channel for grace, a way to dissolve separation and embody unity. In mystical framework, contribution is not just moral- it is ontological: it affirms our interbeing and reflects the divine impulse to create, nurture and uplift.

"The soul grows not by what it receives but by what it gives"- echoes across Sufi, Vedantic and Christian Mysticism.

From secular or philosophical standpoint contribution enriches life by fostering empathy, responsibility, and shared purpose.

Life as Experience and Enjoyment

Many embraces life as a chance to feel deeply, explore beauty, and savor joy. This view appears in secular humanism, indigenous tradition and modern wellness culture- **where pleasure, creativity, and presence are sacred.** Here the people believe that experience to lasting pleasure, sacred presence and creative depth can be achieved even without following the spiritual or religious doctrine- but it requires a different kind of alignment: one rooted in awareness, authenticity and intentional living. They advocate deep awareness without mysticism, seek meaning through creation not belief, pleasure as resonance not consumption, Ethical grounding without religion and awe through science and nature.

Life as a mystery and Wonder

Many people find the life as full of mystery and wonder. Life's mystery refers to those dimensions of existence that remains beyond complete human understanding- the unfathomable source, essence, and purpose of being. To the ordinary person, life's mystery is felt in moments when logic surrenders- the birth of a child, the beauty of dusk, the ache of love. Life is the profound mystery of why we are here, and breathtaking wonder that we are here at all.

While there is not a single statistics of how many people find life to be mystery and wonder, large scale surveys show that a majority of people regularly experience feeling of awe and wonder. The specific percentage depends upon the experience. Pew Research Center study shows 93% of people of America feel a sense of awe at the beauty of nature, 80% feel a deep sense of wonder about the universe, 84% think about the meaning and purpose of life and 74% feel a deep sense of spiritual peace and well being at least several times a year. These high percentage indicate that feelings of wonder and preoccupation with life's mysteries are common human experiences.

In reference to this subject the author himself conducted a survey amongst the village people in Balasore district of Odisha in the month of May 2023. The study group was supplied with questionary form (as below) to provide individual opinion. 98% of the common people were believer of God.

Study Statement (Author)-(Reference 12)

Confidential Statement

1. Name:-

2. Address:-

   Village:- PS:-

   Dist:-   PIN:-

   (Put a tick mark)

3. Are you a believer of GOD? (Yes / No)

4. Which religion do you follow? (Hindu/Christianity /Muslim/ Sikh/Budha/Jain/Others)

5. If you believe in Hinduism do you believe in demi-God/ Goddess? (Yes /No)

6. Which demi-God do you believe in?

   If yes, reason may be

   i) Liberate from cycle of Birth and Death

   ii) removes all sufferings of life

   iii) give you a boon to lead a happy life

   iv) will lead you to enlightenment and supreme bliss

7. Which path of religion do you follow and Why?

   (Jyana, Yoga, Bhakti, Tantra, Karma)

8. What is your experience on Gita Bhagavat?

   i) clear and best of the knowledge

   ii) no full notion only trace

   iii) no knowledge

9. Are you believer of spiritual guru? (Yes /No)

10. Do you know the difference between religious sadguru/ spiritual guru/God?

11. Which is true of the two in Human life? (Birth and Human Life/Death)

12. If soul exist after death of the individual?

    If exist its nature?

13. If Jibatma and Paramtma are related and same?

    Opine in few words.

14. If religion and spiritualism are same or different?

15. If different to which you are attracted and why?

16. Do you give the primary importance to Family life or spiritual life?

17. In which age do you like to be spiritual (Yes /No)

The recent development of postmodern philosophy, great scientific and technological advances (AI, GPT, and genetic engineering) and personal ego are greatly influencing the definition of modern human. Currently the philosophical concept of human in the light of theism is shifted towards the atheism. (Reference 13).

Philosophically, scientifically and spiritually the question is bound to arise "Who am I?". The self-answer maybe I am the human in the first order.

Chapter 3

What is A Human?

The homo sapience is constantly evolving into more and more intelligent being on the earth. The word itself means "wise man" or "knowledgeable man". 'Homo' is the Latin word for 'human' and sapiens is derived from Latin word which means wise or 'astute'. Various definitions are available for human. (Reference-14)

Homo-sapiens sapiens is the sub species that originates from Homo-sapiens. These sub species consist of only modern human and scientific for human. (Reference-15)

Definition

"Any living or extinct member of the family Hominidae characterized by superior intelligence, articulate speech, and erect carriage" (Reference-16).

"A human being, A person; a member of this species Homo sapiens or other(extinct) species of the genus Homo". (Reference-17)

Let me consider science and philosophy of human in first place, spiritual and religious aspect in second.

"The Human" – Biology

Before going in to the intricacies of the science and philosophy of human let me look into the basics of human body. The topic of the biology of human is vast and endless which we are still trying to understand through several researches. As commonly believed human life starts with conception inside mother womb and ends with physical death and passes through various stages of growth and development till adulthood.

Ancient Outlook

a. Egyptian

Before science came into play, notion on composition of human body was subjected to the belief system of the then culture and religion of different societies. Ancient Egyptian period (from 2686 B.C., the old kingdom period, to 343 B.C., end of pharaonic dynasty, which ended with death of the 'Alexander the great') was rich in knowledge of mathematics, astronomy, medicine and engineering. Having advanced civilization, they believed that the body is made up of 4 elements earth, air, fire and water.

b. Greek Civilization

Classical Greek civilization was spread between 5th century B.C.E. to 4th century B.C.E. and also rich in science, philosophy, politics and arts. They believed all matter including body is made up of 4 elements. Earth, water, Fire and Air. Aristotle (384 B.C. E to 322 B.C. E) believed in something deeper and postulated that body is made up of different organs. Each organ carries specific function, the Heart being the most important for circulation of the blood throughout the body.

c. Indian Philosophy

The philosophy on human body is deeply rooted with scriptures like Veda and Upanishad. In Sariraka Upanishad and Ayurveda there is elaborate description and philosophical analysis on human body and its relation to soul, birth and death (Reference-18).

Adi Shankaracharya (around 788 C. E and 820 C. E) (Reference-19) made postulation on the subject and developed two famous treaties, tattvabodha and panchikaranam (Reference-20).

Ayurveda a traditional system of medicine originated in India between 3000 to 5000 years ago. It is considered as an 'Auxiliary text' associated with Atharva Veda. According to its philosophy everything in the universe including the human is made up of 5 elements, (Prithvi, Jala, Tejas, Vayu, Akasha)

Prithvi – earth, elements represent bone, teeth, nail and hair.

Jala – water, associate with blood, lymph and body fluid

Tejas – Fire, metabolic process, digestion, energy production
Vayu – Air, movement of breath and nervous system activity

Akasha – Ether, represent space in the body and channels through which the life forces flow.

This type of concept is also described in Ayurvedic text, such as Charka Samhita and Sushruta Samhita. Charka Samhita originated between 100 BCE to 200 CE (Reference-21) and Sushruta Samhita between 6th century BCE to 3rd/4th century AD (Reference-22).

These 5 elements in our body makes combination forming three Dosas (Constitution), Bata, Pitta and Kapha. These three doses are dynamic forces present in relative amounts in each individual as normal. They are responsible for regulating our mental, physical and emotional process. Imbalance can cause ill health and can be corrected by inducing therapies which include diet, herbal remedies, message and meditation

i.   Vata – air and ether elements are combined to form Vata. It is responsible for normal movement and communication includes nervous system and blood circulation

ii. Pitta – composed of fire and water responsible for metabolism, digestion and transformation

iii. Kasha – composed of ether and water responsible for stability, structure and lubrication

This philosophy is passed down through generations as family inheritance or through general practice. It is still practiced in many parts of the world.

Modern outlook

'The Human' – marvelously designed and unique in each individual. All of us utilizes the same natural and self-created resources for existence. Human body is composed of elements, micro-elements, organic and inorganic materials. During the process of growth and development these are utilized to form cells, tissues, organ and organ system to carry out ultimate activity as when required. About 60% of our body weight is water (vary between 45% to 75% depending upon sex, age, weight, height and other factors). Other elements are oxygen (O)-65%, Carbon (C)-18%, Hydrogen (H)-10%, Nitrogen (N)-3%, Calcium (Ca)-1.5%, Phosphorus (P)-1%, Potassium (K)-0.25%, Sulphur (S)-0.25%, Sodium (Na)-0.15%, Chlorine (Cl)-0.15%, Magnesium (Mg)-0.05%, Iron (Fe)-

0.006% Other trace elements are Iodine, zinc, copper, Magnesium, Selenium, Chromium, Manganese & Molybdenum.

Human body contain cells which are grouped to form tissues of various kinds. Cell is the smallest and functional unit of life form of human. It carries out vital functions such as metabolism, growth and repair. Death ensues when the vital tissues cease to function. Now the scientists have come up the number of total cells in our body. It varies between 3 X 1013 trillion to 5 X 1013 trillion cells.

Robert Hooke in 1665 discovered the plant cell. He named this basic functional unit as 'cell' and outlined their actions. This was the turning point of the science shattering the old philosophical view of life. It made to think about the Human body composition. During 1830's and 1840's M. Jacob. Schleiden and Theodor Schwan published cell theory (Reference-23) and opined that living organisms are made up of one or more cells. The cell is the basic unit of life, arises form pre-existing cell. Many scientists researched on cell theory at molecular and micro-molecular level. In 1953's James Watson and Francis crick proposed the structure of DNA which is responsible for storing and transforming genetic information in all living organism.

From above discussion it is apparent, while describing 'human', that there is difference of opinion between pure science and philosophy. The 'Human', above all, the human life cannot be defined by pure science only (Neuro Science). Philosophically, while describing 'human', inclusiveness of sense perception (Neuro science), mind, soul and spiritual aspect are considered. On the other hand, modern science evaluates the body from functional aspect only. Therapy induced to rectify the human health disorder mostly based on induction of drug or surgery with a view to stop dis-functioning or reverse the process of functioning of cells or organs.

In the post-modern era (after 2000 A.D.) the definition of 'Human' is ought to be changed because of changes in behavior pattern and personality of the human. This change is remarkable due to introduction and wide scale use of internet, smart phone. AI based humanoid Robots (Reference-24) and bio synthetic technology may in future blur the defining margin between biological human and synthetic human.

1: The anatomical and physiological

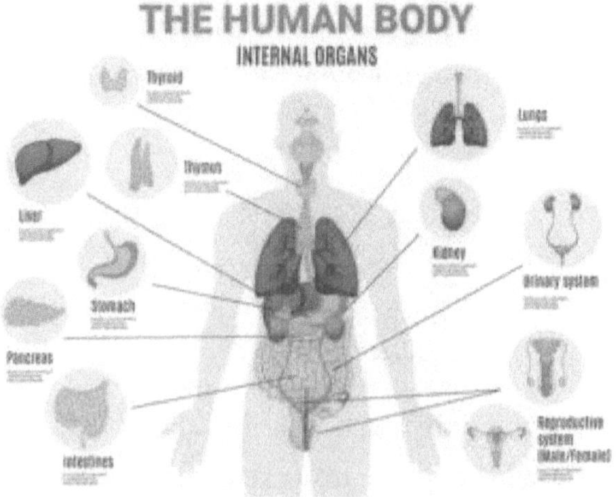

The human body is composed of living cells, tissues, organs and organ system to carry out various functions for existence. The body contains at least 60 detectable chemical elements of which 6 elements, oxygen, carbon, hydrogen, nitrogen, calcium and phosphorus accounts for 99% of the body mass. Though exact no of trace elements present in the body is not confirmed from any source it varies between 10 to 20 numbers. Mostly 17 in number including boron, cadmium, cobalt, Florien, silicon, tin, Vanadium and chromium. The body contents may be divided into organic and inorganic matter as a whole. Organic substances are molecular structures having carbon and hydrogen as components atom. Organic matters are such as

- Carbohydrates – (glucose, glycogen, starch, cellulose)

- Lipids

- Proteins

- Nucleic acids – (DNA &RNA)

- Vitamins – (A, B, C, D, E, K)

Inorganic matters are water, salt, minerals, gases. About 61% of body mass is organic and 39% of body mass is inorganic. Body generally carries out three types of biological reactions.

- Catabolic

- Anabolic

- Enzyme mediated reactions

The work of the body such may be compared to an organized, corporate office where works from sweeper to CEO is divided and responsibilities assigned. Any of the mal functioning of the system is ought to affect the functioning of the system.

The body is divided into various systems depending on physio-anatomical principles. There are 11 organ systems in the human body to maintain vitality, growth, and reproduction. Three systems, the nervous, circulatory, and respiratory are vital as the activities are required for immediate survival. Eight others systems are nonvisual, required for late survival. These are muscular, skeletal, nervous, Circulatory, Respiratory, Digestive, Urinary, Endocrine, Integumentary, Reproductive, Immune system.

A: Muscular-skeletal system: (Muscular and skeletal combined)

Muscular and skeletal systems combined are known as musculoskeletal systems. It involves bones, muscle, cartilage, and tendons that support our typical structure and helps in movement and doing finer to larger activities.

B: Nervous systems

The nervous system comprises a brain, spinal cord, nerve cells, and fibers. The brain is the controlling unit of voluntary and involuntary functions of the body. All the functions are coordinated and maintained by transmitting messages to all the parts of the body (it could be related to the spiritual and kundalini flow of energy).

C: Circulatory system

The heart, arteries, veins, blood, electrolytes, and chemicals are components of the circulatory system. The heat is the vital structure which is singular, auto-pulsating, nerve-regulated, muscular pumping organ, situated inside the chest cage. It receives deoxygenated blood from different parts of the body through veins in the right upper chamber and sends the same to the lung through the right lower chamber for oxygenation. In return, it receives the oxygenated blood from the lungs in the left upper chamber and sends it to the left lower chamber. From there, the blood is sent to different parts of the blood through large and small arteries. Veins and arteries are visible structures. It is appropriate to mention that the spiritual heart (Hurdy) is not the physical heart as described above.

D: Respiratory systems

It starts from the nose and ends at the alveolar of the lungs. Two lungs right and left situated on both sides of the heart inside the chest cage. The first breath when the child takes the air through the nose goes to the lungs through the respiratory tract which leads to opens up of alveoli; the exchange of oxygen (outside air) and carbon dioxide (from blood) takes place by the process of diffusion. Breathing is a vital activity both scientifically and spiritually (Pranayama).

E: Digestive systems

Breaking down of food and substances, absorption of nutrients, and excretion of the unabsorbed products are the main functions of the digestive system. Externally it is visible as the mouth where mastication takes place. Further process of digestion takes place through the stomach, small and large intestines. The nutrients, electrolytes, and chemicals are absorbed through the epithelium goes to the blood. Through blood, these nutrients and chemicals reach the different parts of the body. The mouth and anus are the visible parts.

When describing "The Human" we ought to know the physical and functional aspect first, without which the knowledge is incomplete. This blog is in continuation of past blog 8 in Brief.

F: Urinary system/Excretory System

This system includes series of organs starting from kidney to ureter, bladder ending at urethra. Both kidneys are bean shaped, Right is placed behind the liver, left is behind the stomach and spleen on both side of the vertebra extending from 12th thoracic up to 3rd lumbar below. urine is filtered out when blood passes through the kidney. It is responsible for maintaining fluid, electrolytes and acid-base balance of the body.

G: Endocrine system

It is responsible for the production of various hormones which regulate different body functions including growth, metabolism, and reproduction.

H: Integumentary system

This is most visible exterior organ of the body includes skin, hair, nail and glands. Important functions are protection, regulation, sensation, production.

Sweat gland: regulate the body temperature by producing and releasing sweat.

Apocrine gland: the exact function of this gland yet unknown. It is suggested that it has some role in pheromone production in some animals including Human.

Sebaceous gland: responsible for lubrication of skin and hair by secreting sebum. Sebum has got anti-microbial properties, also helps in preventing skin from up radiation, heat and cold.

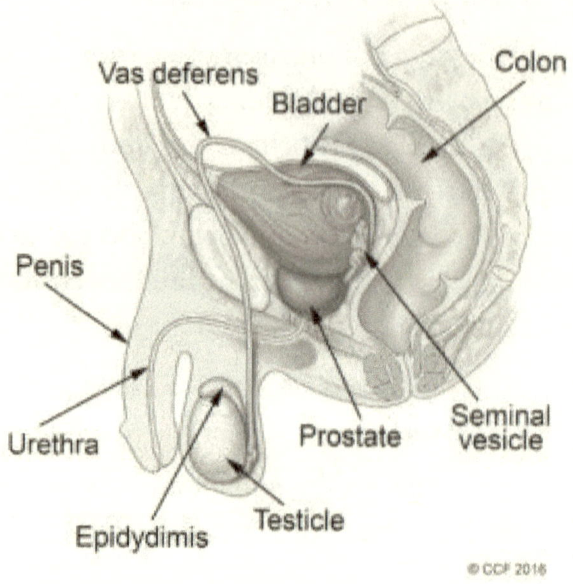

FEMALE REPRODUCTIVE SYSTEM

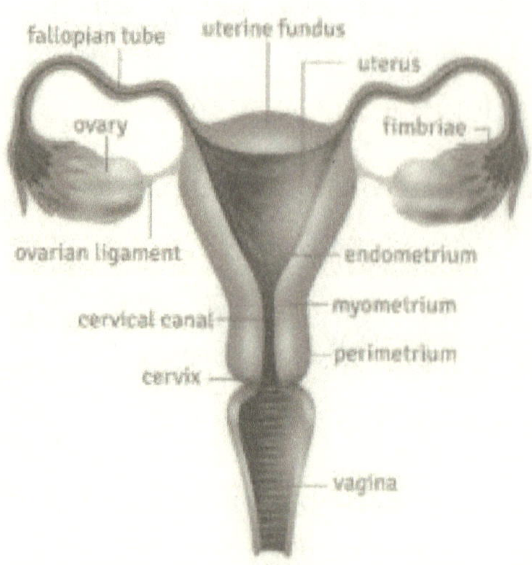

I: Reproductive system (Female and Male)

This system is collection of organs and tissues different in both sexes which work to facilitate sexual reproduction of Human and are inter dependent.

Male Reproductive system includes

Testis -one each side of the scrotal pouch responsible for production of sperm and male sex hormone, the testosterone Epididymis – situate on back of the testis, long coil tube, responsible for maturation of sperm.

Vas deferens – tube for transport of sperm from epididymis to ejaculatory duct. Seminal vesicles – situated at the base of bladder secrets fluid that makes semen.

Prostate gland -situated below the bladder at the neck, secrets milky white fluid that nourish and protect the sperm. Bulbourethral gland – a pair of gland beneath the prostrate that secretes the fluid and lubricate the urethra.

Urethra – the tube that runs through the penis and carries both semen and urine out of the body.

Female Reproductive system

The system is one of the complex system of the human and vital for perpetuation of the human species. It has critical role during development of the fetes for diversity of the species. It includes a pair of fallopian tube single uterus, cervix and vagina.

Ovaries – almond shaped organ on both sides of the uterus. It produces single egg during each ovulation time, responsible for production of female sex hormone mainly estrogenic and progesterone.

Fallopian tubes – a pair of tubes, one on each sides connected to ovary one end and uterus to the other end. Eggs are fertilised by sperms in the tube, which comes from vagina during intercourse. The fertilised eggs are carried to the uterus for the implantation.

Uterus – it is called womb of the mother, where fertilised eggs (zygote) are implanted and develops into full grown fetes. The lining of the uterus sheds blood and other products during menstruation in each month if pregnancy doesn't occur.

Cervix – lower part of the uterus plays a vital role during labour and delivery of fetes.

Vagina – It connects the cervix inside to the outside.

It is a muscular channel through which menstrual blood comes out, also helps in birth of the baby. It is the organ of sexual intercourse.

In addition to this structure female reproductive system also includes breasts meant for milk production and breast feeding.

Philosophically modern reproduction is drawn into controversy due to advancement of knowledge and technology in reproduction. There are argument and counter argument on reproductive autonomy, reproductive guide and reproductive choices. Moral values are analysed now a day in carrying out other reproductive procedures like in-vitro fertilization and surrogacy.

J: Immune system

Immune system is very much complex, integrated, coordinated structures comprising cells, tissues, organs and proteins. Primary lymphoid organ are thymus and bone-marrow. Secondary organs are spleen, tonsil, lymph vessel, lymph node, adenoids, skin and liver. It works for defending or limiting infections invaded by bacteria, virus, parasites, toxins, fungi and cancerous cells.

Adaptive/Acquired Immunity – Day one after birth the baby-body is exposed to outer environment and comes in contact with various pathogens and immunity is produced against each. The body keeps a record copy. When re- exposures happen the body deal with invaders quickly.

Innate Immunity – It is the first line of defence against pathogens. It includes skin and mucous membrane of throat and gout. The response is general and nonspecific.

Passive Immunity – it is temporary type of immunity derived from another person. Through placenta during pregnancy and through breast milk during breast feeding, the antibodies from mother comes to the baby.

WHO has put much stress on maternal and child health in order to make a healthy wellbeing and above all healthy society.

Sometime however immune system may go wrong, mistakenly attack the body's own cell and destroy it. This is called autoimmune disorder Sometimes pathogens are able to suppress or evade the immune system leading to chronic infection. Disease and disorder of health are under constant and progressive research so as to prolong the life and maintain good health. In this respect WHO has come out with definition of good health.

Brain and nervous system

Special consideration of the nervous system is of paramount importance in our understanding of human life from philosophical, scientific, and neuroscience research points of view. Common people attach much importance to this particular system due to accidents, injury and diseases of the brains of course in spiritual principle, the brain is the doorway to connecting the living to the divine. The system has two subsystems. CNS: central nervous system, PNS: peripheral nervous system.

CNS comprises of brain and spinal cord. The brain has three parts. The cerebrum is responsible for conscious thought and voluntary motor control.

The cerebellum is for balancing and coordination of motor movement.

The brain stem is consisting of three-part. Midbrain connects with the cerebrum upwards and down with pons, the middle part. The medulla, the bottom most part connects upward with pons and down with the spinal cord. The function of the brain stem – basic autonomic functions like breathing heart rate, and maintenance of blood pressure.

The spinal cord is a cylindrical cord-like structure starting from the brain stem at the upper level and ending at the lumbar region of the lower level. The vertebrae column starting from below the base of the skull encases the spinal cord and makes a hard barrier.

Peripheral Nervous System

It includes all the nerves that connect the CNS (Brain and spinal cord) to all parts of body tissue including sensory receptors, muscles, and organs. It is of two types: SNS (Somatic Nerve System) and ANS (autonomic nervous system). SNS is responsible for voluntary muscle movement and sends sensory impulses to CNS for interpretation and coordination. ANS is responsible for involuntary actions like heart rate, digestion and breathing. ANS is of two types, the parasympathetic nervous system, and the sympathetic nervous system. The parasympathetic nervous system is responsible for the relaxation and restoration process. The sympathetic nervous system is responsible for flight or fight response.

Definition of Brain

Definition of brain does not imply accumulation of large no neuroanatomical and neurobiological data. None of the scientific framework has decisively passed the test of experimental investigation on most of functional realms of brain. In this context OLAF SPORNS, the famous professor psychological and brain science of Indiana university quotes "Modules of brain networks define communities of structurally and functionally related areas, but they do not represent or support discrete mental faculties."

There are many things about human mind that science does not know. Many occurrences of world phenomena related to humanity cannot be answered by pure science and technology. Technological advances have created much confusion even in minds of guardians of society as happened in the past as well. Recently the whole of the world is apprehensive of AI, because of unpredictable future AI may pose to humanity. ELON MUSK has put it to be more dangerous than Nuclear Bomb. He has quoted," I think AI is potentially more dangerous than nukes." AI is now being used to understand how human think, learn, make decision autonomously. The most remarkable feature of ai of becoming self-supervised learning,

learning from experience. It may so happen that it may acquire consciousness and replace the human mind, others are sceptical for different reason.

Brain as viewed in the mirror of science

Human brain is the most complex organ system, composed of nerve tissues, essential for our survival and wellbeing. It is the seat of intelligence, interpreter of all senses, initiator of body movement, controller of emotion and behaviours and judgement. Human brain is source of all qualities that define our humanity. In this regard there is a beautiful quote by V.S Ramachandran, a neuroscientist and author of 'phantoms in the brain' – 'The brain is a mystery machine, constantly trying to make sense of the world'

Advance scientific and technological knowledge's are applied to explore the structural and functional aspect of NS, brain in particular, to define the modalities of brain activities. Quote by Lisa Randall- "Neuroscience is exciting. Understanding how thoughts work, how connections are made, how the memory works, how we process information, how information is stored – it's all fascinating."

In spiritual context minute details of various scientific research results of NS, brain in particular are not mentioned. Elaborate description of today's research is very vast and mostly based on theoretical principles, philosophy and observations. Glimpse of such research have been discussed in Non spiritual blog. It may be referred in Non Spiritual contents in same site www.divinejourney.org.in.

Studying the Brain

Let's me enumerate in brief what studies of the brain are all about.

NEUROSCIENCE: Vast scientific study of nervous system which includes brain, spinal cord and peripheral nerves. It is a multidisciplinary science which includes Anatomy, Physiology Developmental Biology, Molecular biology, Cytology, physics chemistry, medicine, psychology, statistics, computer science, mathematical modelling. The aim of study is to understand the fundamental and emergent property of brain, neurons, neuronal circuits and glial cells.

NEUROPSYCHOLOGY: It works under the umbrella of both psychology and neuroscience based on principle of Basic science and Applied science. From psychological aspect -Some other branches like Biopsychology, Clinical psychology, Developmental psychology, Cognitive psychology come in to play different roles. Neuroscience aspect – some branches like cognitive science, Behavioural science, Affective neuroscience, works in no relation with psychology.

COGNITIVE NEUROSCIENCE: It studies the biological basis of cognitive functions of brain such as attention memory, learning, language and decision making by using various other scientific methods like Electrophysiology, Neuro imaging, Cognitive psychology.

NEUROANATOMY: It is the study of gross and microscopic structures of brain and spinal cord as well as nerve tissues.

NEUROPHYSIOLOGY: It studies the functioning of nervous system at cellular and molecular level. Studies focuses mainly on electrical properties and signal system of neurotransmission.

NEUROIMAGING: Advanced technology like USG, MRI, fMRI, PET are applied utilising advanced machines to take images of structures and functioning of brain.

NEUROINFORMATICS: Principles of neuroscience and computer science are merged together to develop a tool for collection and analysis and storages of data collected during research activities The vast no of data comes from varieties of sources like neuroimaging, electrophysiological recordings, and behavioural experiments. The knowledge acquired thereof can be utilised to develop new treatment for neurological disorders, to improve cognitive function, to create new technology [Robotic arms] to enhance human ability.

Another goal of this discipline is to build a test model of the brain. This model can be used to simulate brain function and know how different parts of the brain interacts with each other.

NEUROETHICS: Neurotic is a field of study that examines the Ethical, Legal, Social implications of Neuroscience research and impact of technology which may endanger the whole human civilisation. It draws insights from Neuroscience, Philosophy, Laws and Ethics with an aim to understand Human nature, and free will. It makes a guideline for the society on DO and DO-NOT.

Ethical issues pose a big dilemma for neuroscience to go un-Restricted for example: Should we allow people to use terotechnology to enhance intelligence and memory? Should we develop drugs that can alter people's moral judgement?

What are the rights of the people who have brain implants and other technologies associated with?

How neuroscience research influences and changes our understanding of Human responsibility and Free will?

Is it ethical to identify the culprit before offence is done basing on advanced neuro imaging and computational projected data?

NEUROTHEOLOGY: Neuroethology is fast growing field of research activities combining philosophy of mind, neuroscience and religion/spiritualism and tries to solve the unanswered age old concepts. It focuses on neural correlates of religious and spiritual experiences.

Researchers are trying to understand the biological basis of spirituality. They have made some breakthrough by identifying some area of brain responsible for those spiritual experiences. Most recent study was published in the journal of Biological psychiatry in 2021. Scientist used a technic called 'Lesion network mapping' to identify the brain circuit for the purpose. They found that Neuronal circuits centred in the PERIAQUEDACTAL GREY [PAG] is associated with self- reported spirituality. Damage to the PAG circuit are associated with both increase and decrease in spirituality depending upon specific nodes of the circuit that ware affected. They suggest that PAG plays a complex role in spirituality and different aspect of spirituality may be mediated by different part of circuits.

In 2022 a study published in the journal of neuroscience found that PSILOCYBIN a psychedelic drugs increases the brain connectivity in the brain region responsible for spiritual experiences and open mindedness.

Another study published in the journal of frontiers in psychology in 2023, scientist found that spiritual experiences are associated with decrease activity in INFERIOR PARIETAL LOBE [IPL] IPL, of brain is responsible for perceptual processing and self-awareness. Decrease IPL activity may allow people to have more open and receptive experiences of the world which ultimately lead to spiritual experiences. The researchers also reported that spiritual experiences leads to increase in level of grey matter in prefrontal cortex, which is responsible for Executive functioning and decision making.

"When activity in the network of superior parietal cortex [upper part of parietal lobe] or our prefrontal cortex increases or decreases our bodily bound changes"

Proof Giordano explain in an interview for medium.

A study published in the journal of PLOS, in 2023 found that meditation can reduce the activity in AMYGDALA, a brain region involved with fear and Anxiety.

In addition to these above studies there is fast growing studies to prove the link between spirituality and mental health. A review on such idea was published in journal JAMA psychiatry in 2022. They have found that spirituality is associated with a number of positive mental health outcome including lower level of Stress, Anxiety and Depression.

However, the neuroscience of religion is not straight forward. Many logical question do arise. For Instance-How do we measure spirituality and religiosity?

How can we account for individual difference? How to measure cultural differences?

How to avoid the Bias and Reductionism? Even in a reputed NLI institute they say "If you have a brain you have bias" so also in case of reductionism. Some biologist takes reductionist approach at explaining life by reducing organisms and biological functions down to a cellular level.

Neuroethology never explains or invalidates the very existence or meaning of spiritual or religious phenomena. Whether the is divine power behind the phenomena or it is mere interpretation of brain or mere a faith or personal choice?

As ANDREW NEWBERG, the leading neurotheologist says "The most important part is that all neuroscientific studies of religion are ultimately studies of human brain; they cannot prove or disprove the existence of God"

Age old Epistemological question about nature of reality, consciousness and spirituality still unanswered. Unstill we find some answer spirituality and religion are unlikely to go anywhere. The architecture of brain will not allow it.

It is pertinent to mention that the relationship between science and spiritualism/religion needs a separate discussion.

Spiritual Definition of Brain

In 1859 through his published book 'On the origin of Species 'Charles Darwin postulated theory of evolution by process of natural selection. Though the theory is time tested, many of the scientific advances in the discipline of physics, geology, chemistry, molecular biology has supported refined expanded in recent time it has failed to explain the soul. The theory does not explain WHY the evolution occur in first place. Many evolutionary biologists do not refute the presence of God. They believe that evolution is an elaborate description of a process that govern the development of life on earth like many other theories like atomic theory and germ theory.

Spiritual definition of brain still a complex and evolving concept. It can be seen as The brain is a portal to higher consciousness.

It is a tool like, a physical subject, connecting with divine. It is a source for creativity and inspiration.

It is a vehicle for physical healing and transformation.

Brain is a sacred and supreme space where we connect our deepest self with larger universe incomprehensible by common mind. By prayer, meditation ritual practices we open our self to new level of awareness and understanding. Brain can be utilised for spiritual purpose through

Meditation

Prayer

Yoga

Art

Music

Many other functionaries related to brain which are true in spiritualism, found in many religious text all over the world, cannot be proved by science are

A = Nature of consciousness

B = The existence of SOUL or SPIRIT.

C = Possibility of life after death. Is there life after death? What is it like? Where are they?

D = Existence of GOD or supernatural being. The particular nature of GOD. = What is GOD? What relationship does have with humanity. What are GOD's intentions?

E = Meaning and purpose of life

F = Origin of religion. Where did religion come from? How did it start? Why did people have religious impulses? Of course there is proof of religious leaders and messengers born on earth to propagate different religious context and spiritual experiences with almost same philosophy and aim to keep human race going at peace

G = Miracles = Are miracles are real or virtual? If so why do, they happen?

H = Intuition = It is often described as "gut feeling" or a "sixth sense." What the nature and how they occur. Mystics often describe having intuitive experience that provide them with insights in to the nature of realty.

I = The problem of Evil- Why evil exists in the world if there is a loving GOD. Why our mind is subjected to evil?

There are a lot of other religious/spiritual phenomena which are beyond comprehension of normal mind/brain Extrasensory perception. [Telepathy, Clairvoyance, Precognition etc.]

Visions. Ecstasies Mystical Raptures-Stigmata. -Transcendences. Enlightenment. Lucid dreaming. Samadhi etc.

Recently correlation between science and spiritualism is being thought of. People with spiritual practices shows cortical thickening of prefrontal cortex of brain. Right parietal lobe is responsible for defining me, the Ego. It is quieted during spiritual experiences. A specific brain circuit linked to spirituality is being proposed to be located in periaqueductal grey matter of brain. This area reacts in a similar way to diverse spiritual experiences regardless of traditional approach, race creed, gender. Inspire of all recent development nothing is conclusive. Spirituality is broad, has vast experiences in life. It is a way to define the meaning of life.

As German neuroscientist Olaf spurn has put it 'Neuroscience still largely lacks organising principles or theoretical frame work for converting brain data into fundamental knowledge and understanding' In spite of vast no of data accumulation in neuroscience research, and additions of philosophical new thoughts, our understanding of brain appears to be approaching a more confusing and diverse state.

Chapter 4

Human Actions and Responsibilities

What are the human actions?

Human being are the MOST intelligent and biologically active agent, who can create and in fact does voluminous activities. Human actions and responsibilities are two sides of the same coin. As a human we can make choice and judgement and subsequent actions affects himself and all around us Responsibilities are attached to actions to use it wisely and effectively.

How to categories all in to a near consensus platform? Let me discuss a few as below. **HUMAN ACTION**

Human actions are the output of conscious choice or the result of unconscious process or automatic behaviours. The actions may be positive or negative or neutral depending upon the intent and impact they have on others and environment all around. Human actions are driven by complex interplay of factors including motivations, belief, emotions and circumstances. Actions which are not guided by conscious choice are Habits, Reflexes, Emotions, Instincts.

Actions are various activities that happen for different purposes in various domain like science and technology, arts, music, mathematics, environment, natural science, transport, space and under water explorations, even looking deep into the earth surface. Human activities and behaviours are mostly affected by conscience, a powerful psychological phenomenon.

Division of actions clearly depend upon the perspective from which it is seen. Maybe it is divided broadly in to 4 categories, Economics, non-economics, leisure activities, religious and spiritual activities. Economic groups have taken preponderance over others because of its importance in maintaining livelihood. There are overlapping of the groups because of the continuity of the process. I do believe spiritual and religious groups to be given highest honour being the vehicle of peace and joy for mankind.

Human activities divided into 5 categories in different way. (Reference-25)

Primary activities – Those involves extraction of raw materials directly from earth and other natural resources like farming, fishing, mining, forestry.

Secondary action – Activities involves the processing of raw material into useful product such as construction, power generation and manufacturing

Tertiary activities – Providing services that are needed for society such as trade, tourism, transport, education, health care,

Quaternary – Generations, storage and dissipation of high knowledge of information, research, consultancy, internet activities, web designing, AI as well.

Quinapril – These involves highest activities of decision making, administration and governance.

Human Duty and Responsibility

Human duties and responsibilities are the ethical obligations and moral imperatives that individuals have towards themselves, and world around them. These duties and responsibilities encompass a wide range of actions and from respecting the fundamental rights of others to protecting the environment for future generations. Duties can be summarized as:

1. Duties to oneself:

   A-Self-preservation: It is the most important and first duty of a human to take action to protect one's own life and wellbeing, otherwise called self- defines. Self-defines is termed as right to use force to protect oneself from any harm It is a fundamental human right that is recognized in the international law. The laws vary from country to country. It is a complex issue as there is no easy answer to question as to what is considered the humane self-defines.

   B-Self-improvement: One's own duty also include developing own physical, moral and intellectual capacities. C-Self-respect: Duty to uphold own dignity and worth.

2. Duties to others:

   Respect: Duty to treat others with dignity and consideration.

   Non injury: Actions to avoid causing harm to others.

   Justice: Duty to promote fairness and equalities. It is applicable to all self and non-self as well and varies from time to time along the geographical boundaries.

   Beneficence: Duty to act in the best interest of others.

3. Duties to world at large:

    Environmental stewardship: Duty to protect and make sustain the natural world.

    Social responsibilities: Actions to contribute the wellbeing of society.

    Global citizenship: It is rather a Hindu philosophy imbibed in to modern days of 'BASUNDHEBA KUTUMBAKAM'

Duty and Responsibility of Human is defined in a way as "Declaration of human duties and responsibilities (DHDR). Under the auspices of UNESCO, it was defined for the purpose of declaration. It was proclaimed on 8th July 1998 in Valencia, Spain. According to DHDR Article 1 Duty means – Moral or Ethical Obligation

Responsibility means – An Obligation that is legally binding under existing international law.

DHDR has 12 chapters and 11 articles. The whole of the contents is not under consideration here. Moreover, the subjects are more complex. Over all DHDR call for holistic and integrated approach to human action and responsibilities taking in to account the individual, social and cosmic dimension of human existences. (Reference-26)

Setting individual duty and responsibility as separate, the collective actions of the order of global community to be aligned with international formulations. It is to be renewed from time to time and binding to all administrations, local and global to ensure the peace and justice of the planet.

Chapter 5

We, the Human

It is not possible to divide and typify the whole human being into different groups. It will lead ultimately to controversy, complexities, and needless debates. moreover, for classification, some borderline clear-cut feature subject to a particular group is required. Human life is continuous and the expression of different characteristics vary kid of human identity is wide and divergent. Moreover, now a day, scientific activities, thought, philosophy, ethics, laws, and sociocultural life are multifaceted and dynamic, but of course, it is possible to some extent to categorize based on race, ethnicity, language, gender, and above all nationality (I have discussed about different groups of people based on spiritualism and religion in blog 3). Taking different perspectives in light of philosophy and science, humans can be discussed in four ways.

1. **Human being**

2. **Being Human**

3. **Human Person**

4. **Humanism**

1: Human Being

It relates to the basic feature of the human species (homo sapiens and sapiens). It is more devoted to the origin of the human species, genetic makeup, distinct physical presentation like bipedal nature, standing upright on two feet, possessing opposable thumbs, and a large brain. Human have the brilliant speech and communication skills that enable us to express ourselves. Human beings are sentient and conscious (self-aware). Sentient refers to the capacity of an organism to perceive and experience sensations of pleasure, pain, and emotion. Consciousness on the other hand described as 'Consciousness at its simplest awareness of internal and external existence' [wiki] There are lot of opinions about these attributes, can be taken up separate. Human has been provided with developed five sensory organs; eyes for vision, ears for hearing and balance, nose for smell, tongue for taste, skin for touch and sensitivity to temperature and pressure.

The human being possesses a wide range of social, cultural, and behavioral traits that distinguished them from animals. other features include language, articulation of speech, art, music, religion, governance, ethics, and making laws for human civilization. Human has the capacity for expressing emotions including joy, love, and sadness. Decision making another feature of human beings, when done in a good direction makes him noble and if directed evilly, makes his life waste. Human right is another important feature and it is defined as inherent rights and freedom that all people are entitled to regardless of their gender, ethnicity, religion and nationality. This entitlement comes from civil, political, social, cultural, and economic forums. Right to freedom of thought, conscience, and religion

There are many attributes that proves to be human. These are Empathy, Compassion, Morality, Creativity, Self- awareness, Free will. Other important attribute is human do have Meaningful purpose of life which gives us sense of direction and towards motivation for existences Having happiness and compassion, which makes us empathetic and altruistic.

These are some of the attributes that may distinguish us from other animals, but they are not unique or exclusive to humans. Some animals do have some of the traits to some extents or have other traits that we do not have. The gap between human and animal minds [alien's is another topic totally] is not clear cut divisive but rather matter of degree of manifestation and complexity thereof. Therefore, we respect and appreciate the diversity of life on planet earth.

2: Being Human

"Human being", "being human", and "human person" is causally used terms; however, it holds a deeper meaning and should be carefully used.

Differences are "human beings" is used as a noun, and "being human" as a verb." Human being" can be used in scientific terms and "being human" can be used more in an informal context where compassion, empathy, and behaviors need to be implied. A "Human being" is a biological being having all characteristics of the human species. Being human defines its quality as a virtue; It takes as long time as a lifetime of hard work. The human being is not always seen as being human. Individuals with inhuman behaviors are also human beings. Terrorists are not being human. "Free will" is one of the characteristic features of being human. Free will is defined as the power and capacity of humans to make decisions or perform actions independently of prior events or the state of the universe. There is a lot of debate on the "free will" concept and not to be discussed here.

3: Human Person

The great American philosopher Harry G. Frankfurt born in May 1929 in Pennsylvania described that the criteria for being a person are designed to capture those attributes which are the subject of our most human concern with ourselves and the source of what we regard as most important and most problematical in our lives. So the definition of person and personhood is seen more from the perspective of laws, philosophy, and theology. A human may be a person but a person may not be a human!! Human person refers to the moral, spiritual, and social qualities of human beings which give values and identity beyond biology. Some areas of controversies arise when it is argued regarding the personhood of the fetes before birth. If a human is alive and supported by the life support system but unable for conscious decisions. If biosynthetic humanoid robots are capable of acquiring consciousness and doing all goods beyond human capabilities for human civilization. If an alien is more intelligent than a human being and doing all the magnificent work for the well-being of mankind.

4. Humanism

It is a concept developed during 14 the to 17th centuries. Humanism is a progressive philosophy of life, without theism or other supernatural beliefs, that affirms or ability or responsibility to lead an ethical life of personal fulfilment that aspires to the greater good (America humanist association Reference-27).

Humanism is a democratic and ethical life- stance which affirms that human being has the right and responsibility to give meaning and shape to their own lives. It stands for the building of a more human society through ethics based on human and other natural values in a spirit of reason and free inquiry through human capabilities. It is not theistic and it does not accept the supernatural views of reality (humanist international Reference-28).

The philosophical root of humanism can be traced to ancient Greek philosophy led by Socrates, Plato, and Aristotle who placed great emphasis on human thought and action. Today, humanism is associated with widespread atheist belief systems and practices based on secularism, liberalism, and progressive in nature. Essentially, it gives importance to human values, scientific achievements, and creativity. Some humanist groups stress human rights and social justice.

Contradiction to humanist theory is that, it is too constricted on human experiences while a human has limitless probabilities as proved from time immemorial. It fails to take into account the importance of the nonhuman form of life, the broader ecological system of the earth, cosmic phenomena and universe at large. It is just an outcome of a narrow stream of water in a big river like human life.

Chapter 6

Ethics and Ethical Being

Ethics and morality are the twin fabrics that silently stitch the architecture of human conduct and conscience. They, shape our choices, relationship and societies in which we live in. Ethics refers to the systemic study of right or wrong, good or bad often shaped by philosophy, laws, or professional codes. It asks what is right to do. It is a branch of philosophy called moral philosophy. It is the 'why' behind our rules and choices. While the laws tell us what we must do to avoid punishment and social norms (etiquette) tells us what we should do to be polite, ethics ask deeper question **"What is truly right thing to do and why"**. Ethics involves developing standards and principles and theories to guide our action and moral rules. It is universal and analytical and tries to find principle that can be applied consistently.

Morality on the other hand refers to the actual codes of conduct and belief about right and wrong that are held by a person or society. It is 'what' of the good and evil, justice and virtue. It is personal or cultural focuses on specific rules, judgement and values themselves. Your morality is your personal set of belief about what is wrong or right. This is learned by individual from family, culture, religion or community. Morality is like a set of rules by a specific game say it soccer; on the other hand ethics is like the philosophy of a sportsmanship and fair play.

In simpler term

Ethics is reflection; morality is action. Ethics ask

"Why I should?" morality answers "This is how I do"

Both ethics and morality may interact in Human actions.

Ethics may challenge personal morality, e.g. a doctor treating someone they morally disprove of. For example- a doctor whose personal morality is against the abortion influenced by his or her religion, may work within a healthcare system whose ethics (based on patients' autonomy and wellbeing) require them to inform a patient about all legal medical option including abortion. In this case the doctor has to navigate the conflict between the internal moral codes and external ethical framework of their profession.

Moral dilemmas-Situations arises where there is conflict between the two or moral values or principles making it difficult to choose the right course of action for example when one is to lie if that lie save one's life or is it right to lie to protect someone's feeling?

Why Ethics Has Become the Pivot of Action in Modern Times

When the Power Rises Without Wisdom;

In earlier ages, human power was limited by nature's boundaries.; today, it is almost boundless (or if more to be explored). Science has given us the ability to alter genes, reshape ecosystem and even simulate consciousness. But as the power expands faster than wisdom the age turns reckless-strength become blind and progress loses its soul. At that time moral dimension becomes the only compass that can prevent progress from turning into peril.

Knowledge multiplies options;ethics determine the directions.

Without ethics, intelligence becomes dangerous; with ethics, it becomes divine.

As the External Authority Collapse

Traditional sources of moral guidance like religion, tribe, custom once held society together. But in modern global world these are fragmented and no more reflects the pure truth. Humanity now lives amid the plurality of beliefs, ideologies and identities. Hence, ethics must evolve from external obedience to *inner understanding.*

When the pillars of external power fall, ethics rise from within-quiet, personal, and profound. The soul becomes the sovereign.

When Acceleration of Consequences bring Havoc

In ancient world moral actions rippled slowly through small community sometimes faded away. Today a single act has **instant impact** beyond proportion. A single tweet, post or algorithmic decision can ripple across millions in seconds- both truth and misinformation. **Data Exposure** of the whole mankind pose a big challenge. Personal choice once private are now tracked, analyses, and monetized-turning everyday behavior into ethical terrain. This interconnectedness has made ethics not optional but urgent. It becomes necessary to look the ethical front from privacy to dignity. The focus shifts from Protecting data to preserving human dignity in a world of surveillance and profiling. It now shifts the outlook from individual to collective rhythm. Digital Ethics now involve platforms, communities and algorithms not just personal conscience.

In this sense the ethics has become the guardian of humanity's humanity.

When the Artificial and Hybrid Intelligence begin to Outpace the Human

As the hybrid and artificial intelligence begin to outpace human intelligence, the moral and ethical landscape undergoes a seismic shift- one that challenges the very foundation of autonomy, responsibility, and meaning. The emergence of AI, Genetic modifications, and Virtual Realities confronts us with the new moral frontiers;

Redefinition of Agency-

Who is responsible when an algorithm harms the man or machine.? When machines make decision faster and more accurately than humans, the question arises who is morally responsible? Moral challenge will arise when machine begin to decide, whose morality will they follow?

Erosion of Human Centrality

Traditional ethics are anthropocentric, assuming humans are the sole moral agents.AI challenges this by introducing non-human intelligence capable of learning, adapting and influencing outcome- sometimes without human oversight.

As AI surpasses human cognitive task, ethics must confront existential question: What remains uniquely human? What is our role in a world of superior intelligence.

Algorithmic Morality

Can a machine have a moral agency? AI systems increasingly make moral judgements e.g. health care triage, criminal justice, or content moderation. But can a machine truly understand empathy, dignity, or justice? Or does it merely simulate them.

Ethics of Creation

Should we create a life if we cannot ensure its dignity?

Again, in the case of creator of AI, he has to bear the sole responsibility; not just for functionality but for values embedded in design. This includes bias, transparency, and the potential for misuse- especially in surveillance, warfare and manipulation.

When Ecological Awakening Enters a New Phase. The ecological awakening of our age is not just a scientific or environmental shift -it's a moral renaissance, a reorientation of human values towards interconnectedness, responsibility and reverence for life.

From ownership to stewardship. Modern ecological awareness challenges the old view of nature as a source to be exploited. It fosters a moral shift; "we are not master of the earth- we are its caretakers."

Interconnectedness as Ethical Insight. Climate change, biodiversity loss and pollution reveal how deeply interlinked human action are with planetary health. These leads to new ethical principle: "what harms the Earth, harms us all"

Rights of Nature. Movements across the globe now advocate for legal and moral rights of rivers, forests and ecosystems. So, ethics expands beyond human-centric concern to embrace the eccentric values- where nature itself is a moral subject.

Sustainability vs virtue. The, ecological crisis has elevated sustainability to a moral imperative. It is no longer just a policy- it's virtue demanding restraints, foresight, and compassion for future generations.

As the Earth speaks through storms and silence humanity begins to listen-not with fear, but with conscience

When the Spiritual Undercurrent flows- *A moral pulse beneath chaos.* In today's world of hyper-speed, digital overload, and fractured identity, ethics often feel like external rules- fragile and negotiable; humanity senses an inner emptiness- a longing for meaning. But spirituality offers something deeper a sense of inner truth, universal connectedness, and transcended purpose. This undercurrent flows through conscience that choose the right from wrong even when laws fail. That find the impulse to care not as duty bound but by compassionate urge and make realization that individuals are not isolated as being woven into the vast web of life.

The Ethics and morality from the pivot of human action in present day

Ethics today is no longer theoretical philosophy-it is the axis of survival. The human action is increasingly measured not by ambition alone but by the moral and ethical lens through which it is viewed. In a world where every human choice carries planetary resonance, right action is not merely moral; it is existential. In the modern age, ethics must arise as the sacred bridge between science and spirit- a living conscience that guides power with wisdom and progress with compassion.

The Ethical Being

Who is now the ethical in a ever dynamic digital modern world? This is a profound question that sits at the intersection of philosophy, psychology and daily life.

An Ethical being is not simply someone who follows the rules or principle of ethics. It is a person who embodies the deep-seated commitment to moral principles guided by conscience, awareness and a sense of universal good through their actions. It is about who you are at your core, not just what you do in a given situation.

Yet, what is considered ethical in one era or culture may differ in another, because ethics lives in context-shaped by social values, collective understanding, and the condition of human survival.

However, beneath this variation lies universal moral essence: truthfulness, compassion, justice and respect for life. These timeless principles remain constant, even as their outward expressions adapt to circumstances. Thus, while ethics evolve with time and culture, the ethical being remains the same in spirit- one who seeks harmony between inner truth and outer action.

The Characteristics of an Ethical Being

Foundational Inner Attributes (The character)

These are the core virtues that define an ethical person's inner world.

Integrity

This is the cornerstone of the ethical character. It means being whole and undivided. An ethical person's actions align with their values, even when no one is watching. Integrity in ethical being is the unwavering alignment between one's values, words and actions. They are the same person in public as they are in private.

Integrity is the light that makes morality visible

Empathy and compassion

The empathy in an ethical being is ability to feel and understand another's experience as if it were one's own, forming the emotional bridge to moral action. This is the emotional engine of ethical behaviors, moving a person from abstract principle (stealing is wrong) to compassionate action. (I won't take what will cause that person suffering).

Compassion transforms that understanding into a will to alleviate suffering- making ethics not just a principle, but a practice of care. For example; A ethical doctor feels the pain of a struggling patient(empathy) and choose to treat them without payment(compassion)

Compassion is the heartbeat of ethics

Responsibility and Accountability

Responsibility in an ethical being is the conscious commitment to act with integrity, guided by moral principles that honor both self and society. They do not blame others or make excuses.

Accountability follows as the willingness to own the outcome of those actions- facing consequences with transparency and learning from them to uphold trust. When they make mistake, they acknowledge it, apologize and work to make it right. For example- a teacher notices a grading error that unfairly benefits a student. Instead of ignoring it, she corrects the mistake(responsibility) and informs both the student and administration accepting any scrutiny that follows(accountability)

Respect for Autonomy and Dignity

Respect for autonomy in an ethical being means honoring another's right to make informed and independent choices- without coercion or manipulation even when you disagree with him.

Dignity goes deeper: it's the recognition of each person's inherent worth, treating them not as a means to an end but as ends in themselves. A social worker supports a young women's decision to leave an abusive relationship, without imposing judgement or pressure on her and offering resources, safety, and respect for her choices throughout the process.

Justice and Fairness

Justice in an ethical being is the commitment to uphold what is morally right, ensuring that actions restore balance and protect the vulnerable.

Fairness is the practice of treating others with impartiality and respect- giving each person's due without bias or favoritism

The sense of equity is the ethical awareness that fairness does not always mean treating everyone the same- it means giving each person what they truly need to thrive. For example; a judge gives two offenders the same sentence for the same crime, but ensures one receive counselling due to a history of trauma- balancing equal treatment with compassionate justice. *To be just is to see oneself in the other*

Honesty and Truthfulness

While tactful, an ethical being is committed to truth, speaking and acting without deceit, even when it's inconvenient. Truthfulness is the dedication to the facts and reality. They are trustworthy and transparent in their communication, avoiding deception, half-truths, and gossip. For Example; a scientist discovers that her research data contains an error that could invalidate her published results. Instead of hiding it, she publicly acknowledges the mistake and corrects it- upholding truth over reputation. This reflects the integrity, courage, and deep commitment to ethical principle.

Socrates, the great Greek philosopher, chose to speak the truth and challenge the societal norms- even when it led to his trial and death. He refused to recant his beliefs, saying, "***The unexamined life is not worth living***". His unwavering commitment to truth laid the foundation for western ethics and inspired generations to value **moral enquiry over blind obedience**

Courage

Ethical courage is the strength to stand for the truth and justice even when it costs comfort or approval. It is the moral bravery- the refusal to remain silent when silence serves wrong. This kind of courage isn't loud- it's principled. It's what whistleblowers to speak out, reformers to challenge broken system, and everyday people to choose truth over silence. For example; a journalist uncovers government corruption and chooses to publish the truth, despite the threats to his safety and courage. This act reflects the moral courage – standing firm for justice and transparency even when fear and pressure loom large.

Courage is the voice of conscience made visible in action.

Humility

The ethical being acknowledge the limits of their own knowledge and perspective. They are open to having their views challenged and are willing to change their mind when presented with new evidence or a compelling argument. They do not claim monopoly on virtue.

Humility prevents wisdom from turning into pride and power into tyranny.

One of the most profound historical examples of humility as the mark of ethical being is **Nelson Mandela.** After 27 years in prison, Mandela emerged without bitterness, choosing reconciliation over revenge. He invited his former jailers to his presidential inauguration and worked to unite a deeply divided South Africa.

Self-Reflection

Ethics begins with the awareness of self. Self-reflection in an ethical being is the conscious practice of examining one's own thoughts, actions, and values to ensure that they align with moral principles. By that way they continually examines, motives, purifies intention and align actions with higher understanding. They ask themselves "Was that right thing to do?" "Could I have handled that better?" "What are my blind spots?" This, introspection fosters growth, accountability, and integrity.

Kierkegaard, the Danish philosopher, emphasized individual responsibility and inner reflection. He believed that truth is found not in abstract systems but in personal experiences and moral choice. His work laid the foundation for Existential Ethics, urging people to live authentically and confront their own values.

In Essence; The ethical being is not merely a rule follower but a consciousness awakened to the unity, compassion, and truth- a living bridge between knowledge and wisdom, self and society, science and spirit.

Chapter 7

Death, A Beginning Or An End?

With little effort previously I have tried to define, WHAT IS LIFE? keeping the view of biological mortality with/without, spiritual and philosophical background. That is how our actions are reflected and personality is shaped in life journey. So death bears an important land mark in this process. In view of biological mortality that we witness in day to day life human existence is remarkable phenomena. It is quite charming as well as astonishing fact. Individual mortality is an inevitable consequence of life itself. Yet, humanity as species has exhibited remarkable resilience across millennia, overcoming challenges, adapting to changing environments and forging civilization. Death has been designed to bring in to force of natural cycle of renewal, paving the way for new generation to carry on human legacy. In case of biological immortality [As proposed by many by different ways], the world scenario will be completely different.

Through you tube and other social media platform, we can see every day, how people are worried about future. There by society is looking healthy out ward but imbibed with heavy morbidity in mental health and other diseases. But it is important to bear in mind, what is told by many spiritual and religious leaders and special teaching by Bhagavad-Gita, as how to remain calm at all odds of life so as to enjoy a blissful life. In the book "The power of now", Eckert Tolle has explained it nicely. I wish to quote from the book "VIVEKANANDA READER" by him Now, when we study metaphysics, we come to know the world is one, not the spiritual, the material, the mental, and the world of energies are separate. It is one, but seen from different planes of vision. ....'Birth 'life, and death are but old superstition. None was ever born, none will ever die, one changes one's position that is all.

What is death ? How it comes? How does it affect the individual and whole man kind? In my opinion death be it individual or mass, death of any cause [Even death penalty awarded by any state on earth] is the single most universal emotional experiences causing a definite impact in human mind than any other.

Life in particular human life is so vast, precious, joyous, the beauty of which is reflected at any angle it is viewed. It is not comparable to any living object on earth. On spiritual line it is told that everything on earth comes from Brahman, the ultimate source of existence. Everything on earth participate in Brahman as a part the interconnected web of reality. Brahman is the supreme universal realty. As per Bhagbat Gita, Srikrishna reveals that he wishes to be born as human on earth time and again to punish the evils and to establish DHARMA. 'Whenever and wherever there is decline in religious practice, O descendant of Bharata, and a predominant rise of irreligion-at that time I descend myself.' [Gita 4- 7]. It is evident that when life on earth goes wrong, driven by wicked nature of evils, GOD, the supreme manifest Himself to regain the divinity in the society. 'To deliver the pious and to annihilate the miscreants, as well as to establish the principles of religion, I myself appear, millennium after millennium'. [4-8],

Human mind by nature runs from pillar to post to explore its origin and its nature. Studies are going on since our race gets an evolving consciousness, enriched with knowledge through Neuroscience, Philosophy, Psychology, Anthropology, Biology, History, Sociology, above all spiritualism, and religions. Most of the studies reveals only the material science on biological process connecting 3 main dots so to say, the birth, life process, and death.

Birth marks the beginning of the human life, when egg is fertilized to develop in to a viable fetus and is born to the world. The event is accompanied by a series of physiological, Biochemical, and Environmental changes that transform a single cell zygote, containing Genetic information needed to develop in to a complex multicellular, multiorgan human body.

Life process is the time between birth and death. It is the core principle of human existence comprises of Growth, Development, Reproduction, and Maintenance. Based on various studies scientist try to find the reason for such events, affecting good health disease process and death.

Death is the ultimate end of every human life. At individual level each death is different as an event and consequences prior to and after death. Scientific study focuses on objective study of such event and tries to prove everything in terms of neuronal activity of brain. It has failed to explain the vast subjective experiences as well as the principle of consciousness. I have mentioned a few in my previous writing "THE SPIRITUAL DEFINITION OF BRAIN".

Death and Butiful Quotes

Man has believed idea deeply rooted in psychological level, 'Once born is destined to die' [though a few are thinking 0f immortality].

Then why the man dies? The simplest answer may be all multicellular animals die and human being more complex multicellular is ought to die. Let us see what great people on earth define death.

– Some great thinker from earliest time see death as a natural part of Human life.

'There is certain limit to the appropriate length of any time in this world, just as fruits, vegetables, are limited by seasons of the year, everything should have its beginning, its life, and its ending. Wise people willingly submit to this order.'

-Marcus Tullie's Cicero

[Roman Statesman, lived 106 BC to 43 BC]

'The more deeply you understand life, the less you grieve over the destruction caused by death.

-Leo-Tolstoy, Russian writer considered to be one of the greatest Author of all time

[Lived between 1828 AD to 1910 AD].

'Death is very likely the single best invention of life. It is life's change agent'

-Steve Jobs, on 2005 Stanford commencement speech.

[A visionary leader, 1955 AD to 2011 AD, California]

-Death itself is not the end-conclusion, rather makes life whole and complete. =

'In visible world of nature, a great truth is concealed in plain sight; diminishment and beauty, darkness and light, death and life, are not opposite. They are held together in the paradox of hidden wholeness.

-Parker Palmer, American Author from book 'Let your life speak' published in 10.9.1999.

[He is 84 years old still living]

'Death is not opposite of life. Life have no opposite. The opposite of death is life. Life is Eternal.'

-Eckhart Tolle, German spiritual teacher, and self-help Author. He is the author of famous book, 'The power of Now.' [75 years old, still alive]

'It is truly great cosmic paradox that one of the best teacher in all of life turns out to be death'

-Michael A Singer from the book 'The untethered Soul: The journey beyond yourself' published in 2007. [Born on 6.5.1947 still alive]

-Death, an issue of surrender and acceptance =

'If you want to be reborn, let yourself die. If you want to be given everything, give everything up'

-Lao Tzu [Tao-the Chong, Stephen Mitchell version]

[Lived during 6th century BCE, Henan province China.]

'Never postpone a good deed which you can do now, because death does not choose whether you have or have not done the things you should have done. Death waits for nobody and nothing. It has neither enemies nor friends.'

-Indian wisdom, known from uncertain period.

-You are just like a visitor to this planet for a fixed period of time-

'Who brought me to this world? According to whose command do I find myself at this exact place, during this particular time? Life is the remembrance of a short day we spent visiting this world.'

-Blaise Pascal, a French mathematician, Physicist, Philosopher.

[1828 to 1910]

'Regardless of your philosophical beliefs the fact remains that you were born and you are going to die. During the time in between you get to choose whether or not you want to enjoy the experiences.'

-Michael A Singer, from the book 'The un tethered soul: The journey beyond yourself'

= Pronounced psychological effect =

'According to psychology today article, the fear of death can alter many aspects of our behaviours including our fundamental motivation, and actions. Death awareness affects our lives in ways we may not be consciously aware of. [Reference-29]

In addition to this Harvard gazette article suggests that death shapes our awareness of everything else, even when stays in back ground. (Reference-30)

= Philosophical and spiritual aspect =

'This is our big mistake: to think we look forward to death. Most of the death already gone. Whatever time is passed is owned by death.

-Seneca, Roman philosopher, influential personality in stoicism.

[Died in 65 CE.]

'We are not human being having spiritual experiences: We are spiritual being having human experiences.

The quote is attributed to Pierre Telaar de chordin, French Jesuit, Philosopher and theologian.

[1881 to 1955,] Some controversies of course still exist about proper author of the quote.

'Death is stripping away of all that is not you. The secret of life is to die before you die and find that there is no death.'

-Eckhart Tolle.

'Death is but a change of condition. We remain in the same universe, and are subject to the same laws as before.'

-Swami Vivekananda, A Hindu Monk.

'Don't be afraid of death, be afraid of never having lived'

-Swami Vivekananda, A Hindu monk Kolkata, INDIA,

[Lived from 12.01.1863 to 4.07.1902 AD]

'The body dies, but the spirit that transcends it cannot be touched by death'.' Not the body, because it is decaying, not the mind because the brain will decay with the body, not the personality, nor the emotion, for these will vanish with death. Who then remains? Only the SELF, the Atman, the deathless one.'

-Bahaman Sri Ramana Maharishis, The Enlightened being, Tamilnadu, INDIA.

[He lived from 30.12.1879 to 14.04.1950 AD]

'Death is not a blotting-out of existence, a final escape from life; nor is the death to immortality. He who has fled his self in earth joys well not recapture it, amidst the gossamer charms of an astral world'

-Paramhansa Yogananda-

[Born in Gorakhpur, UP, India. 5.1.1893 to 7.3.1952 AD.]

'Life is constant uncertainty. The only certainty is death.'

'Death is a cosmic joke. If you get the joke, falling on the other side will be wonderful'

– Sad guru Jagibasudev-Indian Yogi, Mystic and Author

[Born on 3.9.1957, Mysore, India, still living.

'Death is not something to be feared, but something to be understood.'

-Guru Ravi Shankar

Born in Tamilnadu on dated 13 the may, 1956, Yoga Teacher and Spiritual Leader in India, yet living

Chapter 8

Mortality, Death, Dying

Death? Ah, is it a blow or a relief to living mind. Does it invite any fear and/or emotional instability in human mind now in modern days? Or it is to be accepted as a phenomenon since the creation of world. Man from earliest time might have witnessed death of all living bodies creatures, beasts, and own species. Even in the animal kingdom some of the developed and intelligent species like dolphin, elephants, great apes (of course excluding man) recognise death of their near ones, and shows the typical behaviour pattern towards death and dying. Human being, the most intelligent creation of nature tries to explore every aspect of death and dying by setting new standard of definition produced out of scientific research. Scientific study of death and dying is carried out through a branch of science is called Thanatology. It looks into various aspect of life like biological, psychological, social, as well as spiritual. Various disciplines of science such as biology, medicine, physics, chemistry, psychology are involved in the process, but the current challenge in palaeoanthropology is in figuring out how fossils, archaeology and DNA evidence can be brought together to understand where we came from and exact time of death of various human species through millions of past years, because onetime conclusion is influenced by new development.

The science of death also investigates the possibility of life after death such as near death experience, reincarnation, and the soul. It also helps us learn about the nature of life, the meaning of existence, the personality and humane dignity. But seen through the lens of pure biology, Philosophy, mythology, scriptural thought, and above all, the various religions of the world, different outcomes are seen. Science has failed to answer to all questions as to 'why we exist? and why we die? and why we are mortals?', what is death? how it occurs? And why it occurs. Death history of human is the study of how, why, when human die and their mortality pattern that have changed over time and across the various cultures of world. We can get some knowledge on subsequent discussion.

Analyzing the evolutionary science and different cultures and religion of world we find a sharp difference as to who was the first man to roam on earth and who was the first man to die. At the end of discussion, we may come to a conclusion.

Our Ancesters in Brief

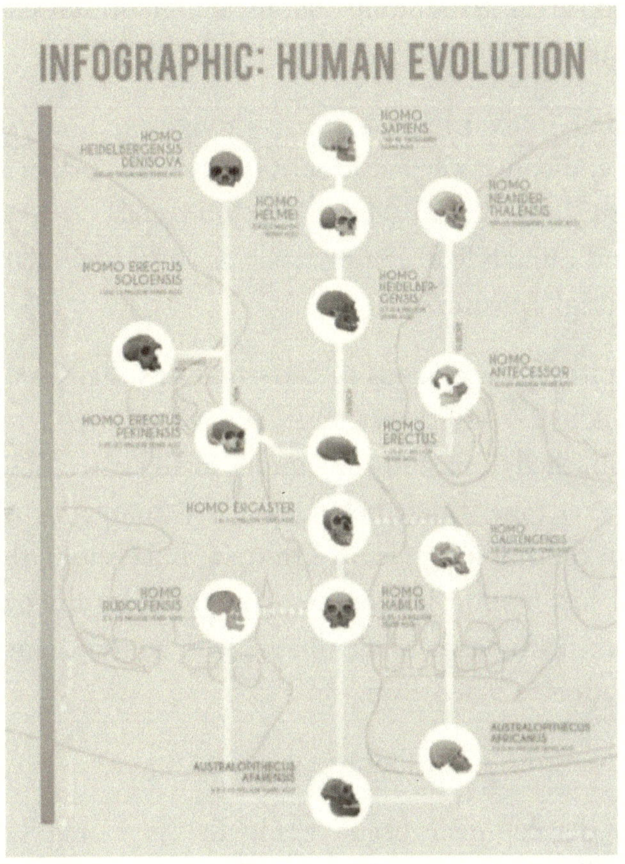

OLDEST known Hominids == Though opinion varies, most accepted candidate is sahelanthropus techadensis, a skull discovered in Chad in 2001 dates back to 7 million years. It has a mix of ape like and human like features, such as small brain flat face, and possible upright postures.

Atralopithecus is a genus of early hominis that lived in Africa between 4.4 to 1.4 million years ago, and gave rise to Genus Homo. This is established from study of Famous fossil named LUCY, a near complete skeleton, which belonged to Astrolopethicus aferensis lived about 3.2 million years in Ethiopia. Lucy shows the features of bipedal locomotion like modern human. Her discovery is the pivotal link in understanding the ancient hominid ancestor and their transition to bipedalism.

OLDEST known Hominids == Though opinion varies, most accepted candidate is sahelanthropus techadensis, a skull discovered in Chad in 2001 dates back to 7 million years. It has a mix of ape like and human like features, such as small brain flat face, and possible upright postures.

Atralopithecus is a genus of early hominis that lived in Africa between 4.4 to 1.4 million years ago, and gave rise to Genus Homo. This is established from study of Famous fossil named LUCY, a near complete skeleton, which belonged to Astrolopethicus aferensis lived about 3.2 million years in Ethiopia. Lucy shows the features of bipedal locomotion like modern human. Her discovery is the pivotal link in understanding the ancient hominid ancestor and their transition to bipedalism.

1- Early Hominins (5 Millions years ago)

Brain development began gradually increasing size so the differentiation of function. Brain volume ranged from 600 cm3 in Homo habilis to 1500 cm3 in homo neanderthalensis.

2- 200,000 Years ago-

Dominant view that archaic humans – usually thought to be Homo heidelbergensis who developed from Homo erectus gradually evolved in to Homo sapiens by approximately 200,000 years ago in either eastern or southern Africa.

3- 100,000 years ago

During this period human became capable of abstract thinking. Innovation and planning for future happened.

4- 50,000 years ago

They developed the capacity for language. The emergence of language played a crucial role in shaping our cognitive abilities and social interaction also marked by complex tool use and symbolic behaviour.

5- 40,000 years ago

Emergence of modern behaviours. During this period cave arts, jewelry, sculpted figurines appeared in Europe. Symbolic thinking and languages likely distinguished homo sapiens from Neanderthals.

Death Definition

- DEFINITION OF DEATH AND DEATH RECOGNITION

There exists some degree of difference between definition of death and recognition of death. Definition is the setting of a standard, while recognition is act of applying that standard to a specific case. For example, a doctor might recognize death by performing specific tests to confirm with the defined criteria.

Recognition on the other hand can be influenced by emotional factors and cultural beliefs. Here is an analogy: Imagine a fire alarm

The definition of fire (rapid oxidation producing heat and light) is similar to definition of death (setting biological criteria)

Recognizing a fire involves seeing smoke, smelling burning or hearing alarm where our cognition factors are involved. Similar situation also involved in case of recognition of death.

- MODERN DEFINITION OF DEATH.

"Death is irreversible cessation of all biological function that sustain an organism. For organism with brain, death can be defined as irreversible cessation of functioning of the whole brain including brain stem. Brain death is sometimes used as legal definition of death."

http//en.m.wikipedia.org/wiki/Deaths

"Death, the total cessation of life process that eventually occurs in all living organisms. The state of human death has always been obscured by mystery and superstition, and its precise definition remains controversial, differing according to culture and legal system."

www.britanica.com/science /death.

Definition of death in early period of human history was not possibly as we define or at least try to define death today. This opinion is drawn from the evidences that so far we have gathered from studies of archaeology, planetology, environmental science, geographical, Genetic studies and other scientific studies on various old cultures. There by the definition of death has entered in to more dynamic and uniformity is lost. millions of year ago when human species was in a nascent stage, death was seen more as recognition or awareness of death and dying rather than a blunt scientific definition as of today. In our search for this process we see some interweaved behaviour's in modern man which might have transmitted from our progenitors.

Brain Death

The irreversible end of all brain activity, including brain stem, even if the cardiovascular system is functioning with external support system, is defined as brain death. It is accepted as death of individual, largely because unlike other organs, like heart, liver and kidney, brain stem cannot be transplanted at least as of now. It is significant to mention that the brain is highly sensitive to oxygen deprivation. The general timeline for changes in brain tissues as

- 30 to 180 seconds -Oxygen deprivation may lead to loss of consciousness.

- 60 seconds- Brain cell begin dying

- 3 minutes- Neurones suffer more extensive damage. Lasting brain damage become more likely.

- 5 minutes-The risk of death becomes imminent, and brain cell begin to die.

In case of cardiac arrest spontaneous electrical activity in the surface of brain disappears within 10 to 30 seconds of cessation of blood flow.

The declaration of brain death involves a thorough examination of a qualified physician, especially a neurologist, who documents the, absence of brain activity based on established criteria. Once a person is pronounced brain dead they are legally dead and death certificate will reflect the date and time when the brain death was pronounced.

In 1959 french physician, Mollaret, and Goulon first described the syndrome of brain death. (coma depasse, a French term that translates to "beyond coma' in English). It refers to a state of prolonged irreversible cessation of all brain activity including brain stem. In this condition, there is complete absence of voluntary movements, response to stimuli, brain stem reflexes and spontaneous respiration. The state is considered equivalent to brain death, an irreversible comatose stage. This coma, depasse, is distinct from other coma in that it is not recoverable unlike other form of coma.

A special committee of Havard School formulated specific neurological criteria to diagnose brain death in 1968. Criteria are, 1. Confirmation of unresponsiveness, 2. Absence of brain stem reflexes, 3. Apnea testing, 4. Exclusion of reversible causes, (that could mimic the brain death such as drug intoxication or hypothermia) 5. Confirmatory test (EEG, Blood Flow studies.)

In 2008, an official statement called 'president council' was presented in which substantiation of brain death criteria is challenged. It is based on neurological research, particularly by Dr D. Alan Shewmon, an neurologist, professor Emeritus in paediatrics & neurology at David Geffen school of medicine at UCLA in Los Angeles, California, USA. He argues that the brain is not the sole integrator of body function and that body can maintain some degree of integration without brain. His studies show that integration of function such as, regulation of body temperature, wound healing, immune defence, and ability to carry out gestation to delivery in case of pregnant women, remain unaffected even beyond the total irreversible failure of total brain at least in some patient who are brain dead. Clinically, at tissue level the pupil still respond to pilocarpine drug 3 hours later, muscles repeated tapped may still responds by mechanical shortening. A viable skin graft may be obtained from the diseased 24 hour after heart has stopped, a viable bone graft 48 hours later, a viable arterial graft 72 hours after onset of irreversible a systole of heart. Shewman's argument is that neurological criteria of death, which focusses on irreversible cessation of all functions of brain do not necessarily equate with death of human being. While his arguments have not led to change the legal definition of death, they have contributed to the on going debate about concept of death and to formulate the criteria used to determine it.

What may be the conclusion as of now? Is it the subtle unknown force deciding the fate of death?

The updated criteria for brain death, also known as death by neurological criteria were accepted on October 11,2023. This was established through a consensus practice guideline, developed collaboratively by American Academy of Neurology, (AAN), the American Academy of paediatrics (AAP), the Child Neurology Society (CNS) and the Society of Critical Care Medicine (SCCM)

The concept of brain death is widely accepted globally. According to world brain death project, there are general agreement on the concept and criteria for brain death despite some variation on some protocol both with in and among countries.

The criteria for diagnosing brain death require the presence of 3 conditions.

1. Persistent coma – The subject must be unconscious and fails to out side stimulation of any sort.

2. Absence of brain stem reflexes – There must be no response in cranial nerves, which control such functions as pupil reaction to light, facial sensation and gag reflexes.

3. Inability to breathe independently – The patient does not breathe on their own, when the ventilator is withdrawn and there is increase in carbon dioxide level in blood.

Brain death is particularly significant for organ transplants because organs, if maintained properly, can be transplanted to a recipient after following certain protocols.

The definition of is challenged based on other several criteria and consideration. Some of the key points are mentioned below

1. variability in diagnostic criteria-

    There is substantial variation in the criteria used to diagnose brain death due to non uniform distribution of expertise, and technology across different countries even within the institutions in the same countries. This lack of uniformity can challenge the universality of acceptance.

2. Assessment of Irreversibility-

    Determination of irreversibility of whole brain function is complex Current definition of brain death require loss of entire brain function including the brain stem. This task is difficult. Now it has become possible to culture brain tissue obtained from a brain dead patient, or resected tissue from operation for in vitro studies. Neurones and glial cells can remain viable for extended period in vitro maintaining their morphological and physiological characteristics.

3. Conceptual and Ethical Implication-

    There are conceptual and ethical implications associated with mismath between legal criteria for death and bedside declaration of death.

4. Technological Advances-

    Technological advances have made possible to maintain bodily function with life support technologies, even when brain is dead, challenging once accepted point of death. Further development can reverse or modify now accepted criteria of death.

5. Philosophical and religious view-

    Different philosophical and religious belief and logic of death are the root social factors influencing the universal acceptance of death criteria. OBE and existence of consciousness other theories are to be proved by science.

6. Legal definition-

    Legal definition of death may not always align with the medical or clinical criteria. This disproportion put a question mark on application of brain death as legal standard.

Therefore, there is need for clear, consistent and ethically sound criteria for the definition of death even if we keep philosophical views away.

Legal Death-

This is an official declaration of death by a qualified authority as approved by the state such as doctor, coroner, or a magistrate based on accepted medical standard and criteria. Legal death must coincide with biological or brain death as some people may be kept alive by artificial support system. The concept of legal death is intertwined with ethical medical and social consideration, and heavily influenced by advances in scientific and medical technology

Persistent vegetative state, (PVS)

Vegetative state is a condition of a person when he is wakeful but lack in awareness of their surroundings and themselves. They may open the eyes, exhibit sleep-wake cycle yet can not communicate to the stimuli meaningfully. It is termed as persistent (PVS) when duration is more than 4 weeks. It is termed as permanent vegetative state if the brain injury is due to non-traumatic and state remain for more than 6 months. In case of traumatic injury for more than one year.

For patient with PVS are not legally considered dead as they have some brain stem activity of maintaining vital function like breathing and circulation without assistance. However they lack cognitive function and awareness. They also retain some autonomic function and potentially can survive for years with medical support. In such situation legal criteria of death, and decision regarding end-of-life care, is highly sensitive. Ethical consideration, high standard medical opinion, law of the land are of paramount importance.

OUR ANCESTORS AND DEATH

Death As Defined By Our Ancestors

Definition of death in early period of human history was not possibly as we define or at least try to define death today. This opinion is drawn from the evidences that so far we have gathered from studies of archaeology, palaenteology, environmental science, geographical, Genetic studies and other scientific studies on various old cultures. There by, the definition of death has entered in to more dynamic and uniformity is lost. millions of year ago when human species was in a nascent stage, death was seen more as recognition or awareness of death and dying rather than a blunt scientific definition as of today. In our search for this process we see some interweaved behaviours in modern man which might have transmitted from our progenitors.

Death and related behaviours as recognized by our ancestors, a scientific look

Death As Defined By Our Ancestors

Definition of death in early period of human history was not possibly as we define or at least try to define death today. This opinion is drawn from the evidences that so far we have gathered from studies of archaeology, palaenteology, environmental science, geographical, Genetic studies and other scientific studies on various old cultures. There by at present definition of death has entered in to more dynamic and uniformity is lost. millions of year ago when human species was in a nascent stage, death was seen more as recognition or awareness of death and dying rather than a blunt scientific definition as of today. In our search for this process we see some interweaved behaviours in modern man which might have transmitted from our progenitors.

> DETECTING DEATH CHEMICALY=

Necromones

Necromones are chemical cues associated with organismal death that are utilised by the conspecifics to recognise and avoid risk of predation, parasitism, or diseases. Necromones signalling appears to be wide spread and likely traces back to aquatic ancestors predating the divergence of crustacea and hexapoda (which include insects) by at least 420 million years. (Specific compounds that constitutes necromones have not been identified yet. necrmones are likely a complex mixture of chemicals rather than a single compound.

A = Volatile fatty acids …. These are carboxylic acids with unpleasant odor, produced by decomposition of organic matter.

B = Amines…. These organic compounds also tend to have strong odors, produced during decomposition

C = Amonia…. Tis gas with very pungent smell another byproduct of decomposition.

Haman and conspecific Necromones.

In humans, the specific necromones have not been pinpointed entirely. Still some candidates are

Putrescine –This foul smelling molecule is produced by the breakdown of the Amino Acid ornithine Studies have shown it can trigger avoidance behaviour in human even at undetectable conscious level.

Cadaverine -Cadaverine is produced from amino acid, lysine through a process called decarboxylation. This process removes a carboxyl group (COOH) from lysine molecule, resulting in cadaverine. Lysine decarboxylase enzymes are responsible for this conversion. Human cells and Microbiome, the bacteria living in our gut, also possess enzyme that produce cadaverine from lysine. The level of cadaverine in a living human are very low and tightly controlled. It is only after death, when normal cellular control mechanism fails and microbiome goes in to over drive. Thereby cadaverine production ramps up significantly contributing characteristic odor of decay.

Research suggests that these necromones interact with receptors known as TAARs (Trace Amine-Associated Receptors) in human nose. When these receptors are activated they may trigger subconscious warning signals that something is dead and potentially dangerous. It is also to note that our reaction to death can also be learned The association of smell with death itself can cause us to react with disgust and or fear.

Hundreds of millions years ago organism evolved the ability to sense necromones.

Among invertebrates, necromones can elicit different behaviours.

Ants, cockroaches, and collembola recognize their dead using unsaturated fatty acids (such as oleic acid and linoleic acid) as necromone cues.

Necrophoric behaviours.

Ants, bees, and termites exhibit necrophoric behaviour by removing dead individuals from from their nests.

Necrophobic behaviours.

Some semi social species instead of removing corpses seal them off or simply avoid their dead or injured conspecifics. Necrophobic behaviours help prevent, spread of diseases or parasites associated with dead bodies.

When did our ancestors develop this awarness of death?

In terms of human evolution, our unique awareness of mortality may have evolved even before our species, Homo sapiens emerged. While we do not have direct evidence for the earliest human specifically sensing conspecific necromones, but it is suggested this ability to detect death chemically likely played a role in shaping our behaviours related to deceased.

Taking the evolutionary history in to account, over six millions year ago, one of our earliest known ancestor, Sahelanthropus, began the slow transition of bipedalism from ape like movement. Homo sapiens would not have appeared for more than five million years. During this extended period various human species lived evolved, eventually died out., intermingling and interbreeding along the way. Therefore it is impossible to pin point the exact moment when our ancestor developed the ability to sense the conspecific necromones. It is clear that our evolutionary journey involved complex adaptations and behaviors related to life, death and memory.

While necromones theory is an interesting thought experiment it is not supported by scientific evidence.

.Necromones are most commonly studied in insects and crustaceans. It is possible that more complex organism might have a more nuanced system for detecting death but necromones would still play a role. For example in case of crickets studies have shown that they avoid areas treated necromones which suggest that these cues serve as warning of danger or an unfavourabl environment.

Death and related behaviours as recognizesed by our ancestors, a scientific look --

How our ancestor recognised death? What was the bahaviour pattern in various time line spanning millions of years. Taking evolutionary concept in to account our consciousness is ever expanding, and showing improving intelligence. We correlate death feeding various cues to the mind, and then draw the conclusion of death. Necromones would not necessarily be the only way our ancestors detected death. Because up to today there is no scientific data suggesting a human specific chemical exists. Even without specific necromones there are several other signs that would have been evident.

:Visual cues. Absence of movement, body stiffness and changes of skin colours would have been clear indicators of death.

:Physical signs. Lack of response to touch or stimulation would have been a strong signal.

:Odor. Besides con specific necromones decomposition does produce a distinct odour that would have alerted our ancestor about death of own group member.

:Behavioral changes. Animals associated with carrion (vulture, flies) might have been as cues to locate the dead.

Necromones, if they existed would have been one additional layer of information for early humans to confirm death. It is likely that a combination of these factors not just necromones, helped our ancestors identify deceased members of the group.

Paul Pettitt, a durham university archaeologist, having special interest in origin and nature of of palaeolithic art and mortuary activity, chronometry, proposes 4 step process for development of funerary custom establishing that our early ancestor did recognise death as the ultimate end of their group members. 1. Chemical detection of death, 2. Introduction of emotion, 3. Symbolic Mortuary behaviours 4. Elaborate customs &Rituals.

> Introduction of emotion—

Some smart social creatures show their emotional response to loss of their own group members or their offsprings.

Corvid birds like magpies squaking alarm calls while gathered around corpses.

When an elephant dies its family and friends gather around to mourn. They attest the death, and touch the body, caress it with their trunks, and make a deep rumbling noise. They even show funeral affair by not leaving the body for hours even for days. Some scientists believe that elephants have deep understandings of death- they know that individual is gone and will never return.

Dolphins also display intriguing behaviour towards their dead, known as "postmortem attentive behaviour". When one dolphin dies, others pause as they pass by almost confirming its demise. If encouraged to move past without stopping, they resist and return to the deceased animal. Their typical behaviour suggest that they understand mortality. it becomes difficult to relate death in emotional terms.

Our closest relatives chimpanzees also exhibit various emotional behaviour pattern to the death of their member. After a wild chimp fell fatally from a tree primatologist witnessed its group members holler, slap the ground, rip up vegetation, throw rocks, embrace each other.

Discover| planet earth by Bridget Alex (Feb 11 2020 11.20 pm)

In a different case of incidence of death, the group members quietly gathered around the dead juvenile. Mother used a grass stem to clean its teeth,

This show up of emotion is 2nd stage in 4 stage process of evolution of recognition and behaviour from early hominins to the late upper palaeolithic period, towards death as proposed by paul Barry Pettitt. The British archaeologist and academic, Durham

University, proposed this long term model of the human mortuary activity in his book, The palaeolithic origins of Human Burial.

In a review in 2018 of these behaviours scientist concluded that with experience and age the apes learned that death is the final event in life, and individual will not wake, but there is no indication that they understand its inevitability- that all animals including themselves, will die. "Where as we fortunately or unfortunately, are aware of it" says study author James Anderson, a primatologist at Kyoto university. He continued, "That may be one of the cognitive differences between us and other great apes'. Pettitt agrees and thinks this awareness led to the evolution of third in his 4 stage process: Mortuary behaviours, which is exclusive to Hominins., If evolutionary biology is to be believed, human are the descendants of great apes. So it is logical that the emotional reactions and behaviour pattern of modern man happens to be quite different from our ancestors.

Paul Pettitt's 4 stage model of evolution of mortuary activity.

1. Initial stage: Stage of Minimal Mortuary Behaviour

   Early hominins likely had minimal or no deliberate mortuary practice. No evidence of intentional burial or ritualized treatment of the dead.

2. Second stage: Emergence of burial practice

   Neanderthals and early modern human (homo sapiens) began to bury their dead intentionally. At the beginning simple burials such as placing dead bodies in shallow pit and covering them with soil emerged.

3. Third stage: stage of Ritualization and Symbolism

    Emotional and belief system entered in to the practice. Burials became more elaborate and ritualised. Grave goods and offerings like red ochre, personal ornaments and tools were placed with deceased. These are believed to be their concept of afterlife, spiritualism, and emotion.

4. Complex Rituals and artistic Expression

    As a play of intelligence sophisticated mortuary practices evolved.

    Artistic expression like creation of cave art, hand stencils and engraving

    Symbolic Burials Intricate grave structures were done. body positioning, specific orientation of dead was symbolic.

    Social significance evolved In parallel with time. These burials signified social roles and status and community cohesion of early human.

    Mortuary Bahaviour

It is defined that mortuary behaviour is exclusive to hominins (human and our closest archaic relatives). Our ancestors developed consciousness that mortality, for that matter, the death is the ultimate fate, (this belief still exist in modern days) to bod farewell and to ease the emotional toll. They made elaborate arrangements for final bid depending upon the concept of life, and after life Some time later on, religious rituals were seen to be involved as revealed from various studies.

The evidence of behaviours pattern and afterlife concept related to death can be found from documents of death from earliest period till modern days from various sources. These are

1- Archaeological evidence

* Cave painting and rock arts.

* Ancient civilisation and burial practice.

* Art and literature like ancient Egyptian art

2 * Prehistoric sculptures

3 * Written Epics.

4 * Wills and Testaments.

5 * Modern days keeping of records.

1- ARCHAEOLOGICAL EVIDENCE

• 	* Cave painting, and rock Arts

Death and rituals related to death of our ancestors can be found from the archaeological evidence of cave painting, and rock arts. Pin pointing the earliest ritualistic death practice from rock arts is difficult some conclusion can be drawn from art form that offer insights in to the early belief and practices towards death.

Cave painting are a type of parietal art found on the walls and ceiling of the cave.

The earlist known cave art was not created in a cave at all. It was drawn on a rock face in south Africa approximately 73,000 years ago predating any known cave art.

A study in 2018 claimed oldest example of non figurative cave painting by Neanderthals, an archaic human subspecies, found in 3 caves of spain, Maltravieso, La Pasiega and Ardales dating to 64,000 years old.

Chouvet cave art in France dating 36,000 years back depict a scene of a man laying on the ground with a bison standing over him. It possibly indicate the haunting accident or symbolic ritualistic sacrifice related to death and afterlife. Though not found art depicting death rituals the presence of hand stencils and deliberate placement of painting suggest a possible connection to spiritual belief and practice.

Another human action of our ancestor related to death is exhibited in cave art form found is the shaft scene in Lascaux cave in France dating about 17,000 years ago. It shows a man with a bird like head falling backwards with a spear in chest while a wounded bison and a rhinoceros face him. Some interpret as the representation of a Shamanic journey or a mythological story.

In more recent times some cave arts depicts the human warfare and violence. This is evident from the painting of battles and Execution in the Serra-da- Capivara national park in Brazil. Dating back to 10,000 years ago painting shows human fighting with Spears, Bows, and clubs as well as scene of torture and decapitation.

- * Ancient civilization and burial practice.

Shanidar cave of Iraq is reveals the oldest burial practice by NEANDARTHALS, dating back to 70,000 years ago. It contain remains of 9 Neandarthals some of them buried with pollen suggesting the flowers were deliberatly placed hinting at ritual practice at death.

Some prehistoric burial practice are found in the cave burials.

Chatalhoyuk Turkey, (PPNA) – This site dating back to 9000 years ago, exhibits remarkable neolithic and chalcolithic proto-city settlement with intriguing burial customs. They involved intramural inhumation, where bodies were buried with in settlement. Numerous houses with burials beneath the floor. This suggest a close connection and behaviour pattern between living and dead.

Elaborate grave goods including organic remains were found in excellent state.

Some burials were linked to scenes depicted in wall painting showing vultures pecking at humanoid figures. The inhabitants of catalhoyuk practiced a unique burial custom of painting the skeleton. The bones were partially painted with red ochre, cinnabar (for males) and blue/green (for females) This tradition applied to all genders and all ages. Including childrens.

Ancient civilisation

- Egyptian pyramids

  These iconic structures, the oldest one dating back to 2630 BC at Saqqara built for third dynasty 's king Djoser reveals the then Egyptian belief system of dead and afterlife concept.

  Egyptian believed that individuals would continue to exist in the afterlife. So they used to mummify the dead, kept grave goods like Jewelry, food, games, and other offerings along with them to ensure immortality. They believed that these items would need in afterlife.

- Mousoleum at Halicarnassus

  This massive tomb built in 4th century BC, considered one of the seven wounders of the ancient world. It exemplifies the elaborate funerary architectures of the ancient Greek, and their believe in honouring the dead.

- Chinese Terracotta Army

  This vast collection of life sizes terracotta figures dating back to 2,200 years back were buried with the first Qin Emperor to accompany him in after life. It showcases the elaborate burial rituals of the Chinese imperial court.

Hindu Believe System And Open Air Cremation

Oldest known instance of cremation is found at Near East dates back to 7000 BCE. It was discovered at the neolithic site of Beisamoun in north Israel. In this cremation pit the remains of a person who died some time between 7013 and 6700 BCE were found. The body was intentionaly incinerated as a part of funerary practice.

Archaeological finding are seen by unearthing cremation site, with burnt remains and funerary objects is a strong indicator of cremation practice. Indus Vally Civilisation sites dating back to 3300 BCE to 1300 BCE, show evidence of cremation.

The practice of open air cremation has ancient root in Hinduism. According to VEDAS (estimated to be composed between 1500 BCE and 900 BCE), the oldest of all Hindu scriptures cremation is considered as a sacred rite. It endorse cremation is a way for body's elements to return to nature – a harmonious completion of life's cycle. In Nepal open air cremation is believed to sever any emotional attachment of the soul with the body so that the soul is allowed to move on from this earthly existence. Practice is often carried out at the bank of river in India especially at bank of River GANGA.

- * Art and Literature

Depiction of death in art and literature from earliest periods till modern days reflects the changing attitudes towards mortality and afterlife concept. Extensive funerary art adorns the tomb and sarcophagi showcasing the complex belief about after life journey. It spans the vast period from pre dynasty period (6000 BCE) to old kingdom period (2613 BCE). Funerary art was standardized under royal patronage, throughout entire span of ancient Egyptian civilisation, the Old kingdom period (2613 TO 2181 BCE), the Middle (2181 to 1570 BCE), New kingdom period (1570 to 1069 BCE). It represents various aspects of death depicting the religious rituals, mythology, and afterlife belief.

Ancient Roman and arts

Ancient Roman arts were seen both during Roman Republic (509 BCE to 27 BCE) and Roman Empire (27 BCE to 476 CE). Roman funerary arts provide fascinating insight into the commemoratioin of life and death in ancient Rome. Funerary monuments were common to both elite and those out side Elite. Pompa, an elaborate, dynamic affairs involving mourning rituals, washing, anointing, displaying the deceased body on an elaborate bier before transport to the tomb or cremation site. Romans both practiced both cremation and inhumation.

2-Prehistoric Sculptures

The Venus of Hohle Fels, an upper palaeolithic figurine made up of mammoth ivory is the oldest undisputed example of a depiction of a human being, found in Hohle Fels Cave, near Schelklingen, Germany dating back to 42,000 to 40,000 years ago. It is now housed at prehistoric museum of Blaubeuren. The Venus of Hohle Fels stands as a testament to our ancient ancestor's creativity and symbolic representation of humanity.

Venus's figurines – These are small female figurines found across Europe are dated between 35,000 to 30,000 years old. The significance of creatin though not very clear it is thought to be a representation of fertility and continuation of life, implied from Exaggerated breast and belly and buttock.

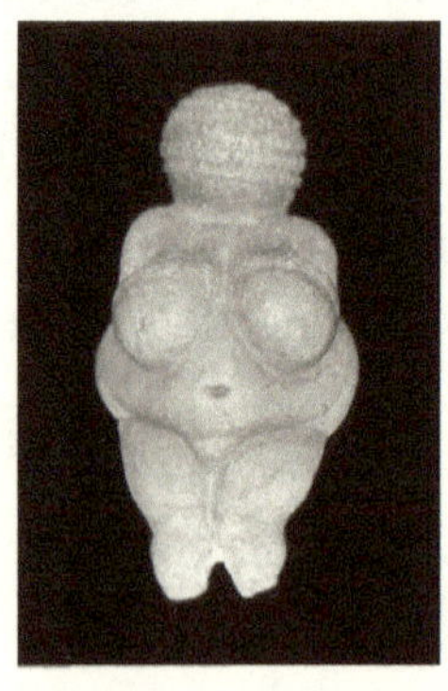

The remarkable Huastec Life-Death Figure is the fascinating example of a figurine, that embodies the interplay between Life and Death. This remarkable sculpture was created by Huastec people who inhabited in the region of North Veracruz, Mexico, between 900 CE to 1250 CE. The most striking aspect of this sculpture is its juxtaposition of a serene young man on one side with a grotesquely expressive skeleton on other side. This duality represent the close relationship between Life and Death in Mesoamerican culture.

3-WRITTEN EPICS

- = While formal writing had not yet emerged prehistoric human expressed them selves through oral tradition, chants, and stories passed down through generations

- = Poetry, music and dance were integral part of the cultural practice.

- = Material arts such as painting, sculpture, drawing, pottery, and bodily adornment also played a crucial role in manifestation of human activity.

The Epic of Gilgamesh is considered as one of the earliest, dates back to 2100 BC 1800 BC to surviving works of literature that offer insight to the cultures and beliefs of Sumerians, an ancient civilisation that thrived in Mesopotamia. The epic began as FIVE Sumerian poems about Gilgamesh, which later combined in to an Akkadian poem. The Epic of Gilgamesh is a timeless tale that explores love, loss, friendship, and quest for immortality, and a search for a meaning in the world where mortality is inevitable.

Medieval 'Dance of Death"

It is also known as, Danse Macabre, is an artistic allegory that appeared in the late middle ages. Little known about the sources. Some scholars connect it to earlier idea of death personified as poems in 13th or early 14th century. Visual depiction of fully developed dance of death concept is a series of painting from 1424 to 1425 found in cemetery of innocents in Paris. In this haunting depiction death summons representatives from all walks of life -Pope, Emperor, King, Child, Laborer. – to dance together towards the Grave. These macabre scenes served as memento mori, reminding the people of life's fragility, and vanity of earthly glories. The danse Macabre was enacted at village pageants and court masques, with people dressing up as corpses from various social strata.

4-WILLS AND TESTAMENT

Those legal documents offer insight in to the lives and death of individuals as well as their belief about afterlife. However the wills are recent invention. So there aren't any records of wills referring to self declaration of death in ancient world. Worth mentioning is Egyptian Book of Dead, which contain funerary texts that specify what deceased hope will happen in the afterlife. Similarly some viking sagas describe how a person wanted to be buried. Viking sagas was prevalant as oral tradition during the period 793 AD to 1066 AD. Icelandic settlers began writing down these oral traditions (12th to 14th centuries AD), creating Viking Sagas as we know today.

During old kingdom period (2670 BCE to 2181 BCE) early Egyptian developed concept of afterlife and used pyramid text on the walls of pyramid for Pharaoh's journey. In 1700 BCE, The Book of Dead begins to take shape in Thebes, combining elements from pyramid and coffin texts.

The oldest testament regarding human birth and death found with in Hebrew Bible, also known as Tanakh, (which are Dead Sea

Scrolls containing biblical texts, dating back to 3rd century BCE) in Judaism. The very first book of Hebrew Bible, GENESIS, contains the earliest account of human life and death. Ther is controversy over the composition date of Hebrew Bible. Scholars generally generally place the date between 10th and 6th centuries BCE.

Hinduism does not traditionally rely on written testaments like other religion. However there are ancient Hindu texts like, The Vedas, (Rigveda, 1500-1200 BCE) Upanishads (800-400 BCE), which, entails the profound aspect of life and death of human.

How Can We Establish The Human Ancestor's Death And Death Related Bahavours

It is quite interesting to ask a question as (I had mentioned in my early writing) to who is the first man to roam on earth and who is the first man to die? In this regard the science of evolution differs quite diagonally to various religious and mythological narration. (both will be discussed in spiritual con text in 2nd volume. The earliest evidence of human birth, for that matter death, comes from various sources, when compiled gives us a clue of death of early human. The scientific studies which includes Biological anthropology also known as physical anthropology – This particular branch delves into Human Evolution, Genetic variation, and Adaptation. Human evolution is studied with in the context of human culture and behaviours. Death being a event in the process leave some foot print in time.

1. PALEOPATHOLOGY-

    Study through ancient individual bones and Reeth to identify the cause of death as disease or physical injury.

2. FORENSIC ANTHROPOLOGY-

Determines the individuals age at death and tries to elicit the cause of death.

3. EVOLUTIONARY BIOLOGY-

Study of Evolutionary history of human and their ancestors. Evolutionary biologist can draw inferences about the pattern of survivals adaptation and existinction. Genetic studies are included in to the cariculam.

4. ARCHAEOLOGY-

Study of human behaviours through material culture plays a central role in understanding the lives and death of our ancient ancestors. It gather biological information from material remains and establishes the link of diet, possible habit and migration. Burial practices and rituals of death reveals insight in to the belief system Emotional response to the dead, and social relationship among the living.

5. PALAEONTOLOGY-

It is the scientific study of life that existed prior to and sometimes including the start of HOLOCENE EPOCH (roughly 11700 years before present days) It examines the fossils to classify organism and interaction between themselves and with environment. Palaentology lies at the intersection of biology and geology but differs from archaeology in that it excludes the studies of Anatomical modern human. It takes help of other scientific technique from mathematics, Biochemistry, Engineering.

It is to note that all these studies does not agree upon a single platform of opinion

Chapter 9

Enigma of Death

Enigma of death seen through the lens of science and philosophy, (keeping spiritual aspect separate for time being) reveals both divergent and synergistic opinion.

Science perspective

Scientist all with modern knowledge prove the physiological process and mechanism of body functioning from cellular breakdown to organ failure that ends in death. But the biological complexity are many and unreached. Life and death are not binary states; they exist in a spectrum. Cells are constantly re generated and also die in a living organism. Understanding the intricacies of ENTROPY- tendency toward disorder, aging, apoptosis (programmed cell death) and cellular turn over adds to the complexity to our understanding.

- Cessation of life is the next enigma. mystery is the occurrence of exact moment of death, and the precise line between life and non-life. Advanced resuscitation and Suspended Animation (HAVE BEEN EXPERIMENTED IN HUMAN ALSO), blurs this line.

- Shifting of goal - Our advanced knowledge, and technology potentially delay and in some cases prevent death. So immortality issue is a real challenge.

- Near Death Experience - NDE (OBE) Documented evidences of NDE, OBE and other supernatural phenomena suggesting a transition phase between life and death. Enough is not said in the mechanism of such happenings.

- Quantum uncertainty - Quantum physics raises the intriguing question about the nature of reality and uncertainty impact on life and death, including possibility of existence of consciousness beyond the physical body.

- Cosmic Ego – To prove or disprove the existence of consciousness beyond human physique is another challenge. According to cosmic Ego theory after death the individual consciousness merges with the universal consciousness.

Philosophy

- Pin pointing the definition of death – Philosophers are confused to define death exactly. Simply scientific definition of cessation of life process is not enough. In phenomena like suspended animation and complex metamorphosis (caterpillar to butterfly) could there be a state where life is suspended temporarily without true death. These raises question about what constitutes 'being alive"

- The unknowable Experiences—

  Death is ultimate unknown in known world. We can not directly experience what it is like to be dead. Lack of first hand knowledge makes it difficult to even imagine what death entails. It is a experiential blank. Is there something more or something beyond our comprehension.

- Alternate Exit- Philosopher ponder whether human can find other way to exit life without conventional process of dying.

- Existential Enigma-Death shapes our existence, influences our choices, and give meaning to life. Heidegger's concept of 'Being-toward- Death' emphasizes that our awareness of mortality define our existence. It is not merely an event at the end of life but an essential aspect of being.

According to Fred Feldman death is a double Enigma.

The first Enigma = Defining death simply as 'cessation of life is not enough.' Consider the suspended animation or future scenarios when the organisms might be revived after appearing dead. Situations challenge the strait forward definition.

The second Enigma = Even if we perfectly define the death it remains still mysterious because we can not experience it directly. We can not know what it is like to be dead. This lack of firsthand knowledge makes death a unique and perplexing.

Dying

Dying is used both as noun and adjective, if so how to define the dying.

"CEASING TO LIVE; APPROACHING DEATH; EXPIRING:"- Adjective

Dictionary.com

'The act or process of ceasing to live, ending, or drawing to a close'- Noun.

Collinsdictionary.com

Earliest known use of the verb die- is in the middle English period. (1150 to 1500)

Death and dying though interconnected meaning and purpose are different. Death is a noun refers to permanent cessation of all biological function that sustain a living organism. On the other hand dying is a verb which means ceasing to live or passing away. So in essence death is the final outcome while dying refers to the process leading up to it.

Dying is a complex process, involving physiological changes, social detachment psychological shifts at the end cessation of all. To better understand this complex process it is categorised to Physical death, Psychological death, and social death.

1. Physical Death

    This aspect refers to physical decline during the process of dying. About 40 to 90 days before death physical changes begin which include reduced appetite, thirst, increased sleep, weight loss and mild sense of happiness. Changes in breathing, circulation, colour, and patient become unconscious, before 'lets go' of life.

2. Psychological death

    This refers to the emotional and mental aspect of dying. As death approaches individuals may start to withdraw and reflect, accepting their mortality and separating from the world. It also involves coming to terms with mortality, experiencing grief, and facing existential question. Individuals grapple with their mortality and have impact on their identity and relationship.

3. Social Death

    Social death occurs when an individual is no longer recognized as a part of social fabric. It involves loss of social roles and relationship and social connection.

Significance and importance-

Significance of death and dying is.

That it is recognised as both inevitable and irreversible.

Through out the entire human history it is regarded as final event in life with social significance.

Every culture has the role to play and every one is different. Religious and cultural beliefs shape practices, rituals, and custom related to death. Recognizing signs of dying allows for better preparation and informed decision making regarding care and also treatment. It is to remember that these dimension of death do not align chronologically. Psychological death can happen before or after physical death.

Mortality and Death

Mortality is defined as ": the quality or state of being mortal " Marriam Webster. "the state of being subject to death' Oxford Language.

Death and mortality are closely related concept at the same time bear different meaning. Death refers to cessation of life an event of transition from existential to non existential state. Mortality on the other hand a condition being mortal, a fundamental aspect of life. Death has many aspect as we have discussed earlier, predominantly having Biological and Philosophical values where as mortality has Statistic and psychological importance. Awareness of mortality can shape our perspective, purpose and legacy in life. In medicine it is used to calculate death rate.

Mortality rate is calculated by various approach. WHO approaches mortality rate

- Estimated General Mortality Rate; This refers to the total no of deaths in a population segment (defined by age and/or sex) divided by total population, expressed per 100,000 people per year.

- Crude Death Rate; This is another way to measure mortality taking the number of deaths per 1000 population in a given year. It is simple measure but does not account for age / sex difference io to account.

Out of 8.1 Billion of world population in 2023 total number of death was, 60,760,150 ((32,662,050 were male, 28,098,100 were female). Adult death was (15 years above) was 53,805,459. During the same year approximately 134 million babies were born out of which 61 million died resulting in net population increase of 73 million a net growth rate of .91%

Mortality in great Epidemics that world has seen.

- **THE BLACK DEATH**, a devastating bubonic plague caused by Y. PESTIS, occurred in Europe from 1346 to 1353. During this period 50 millions of people died which may have accounted for 50% of Europe's 14TH century population.

- **THE SPANISH FLU** pandemic that occurred between Feb 1918 and April 1920 is also called the great influenza epidemic, was caused by H1N1 Influenza A virus. The earliest documented case was in march 1918 in the state of Kansas of USA. Two years later nearly a third of global population almost 500 million people had been affected by four successive waves. Estimated death was not properly recorded still amounts to 50 millions and some rough estimates to even 100 millions, making it the deadliest pandemic in human history.

- **SMALL POX** is believed to have infected human around the time of earliest agriculture settlement some 12,000 years ago. Earliest death due to the disease included SIX EUROPIAN MONARCHS including Louis 15th of France in 1774. In 18th century EUROPE an estimated 400,000 people died annually from this disease. Disease is estimated to have killed up to 300 million people in 20th century, and around 500 million in last 100 years. SMALL POX HAS BEEN DECLARED AS ERADICATED since 1980 making it the only disease to have eradicated so far from planet.

- **COVID PANDEMIC**, caused by the SARS-COV-2 virus was first identified in Wuhan, China in December 2019. WHO declared a global pandemic in march 2020. As of July, 2024 there have been 7 million conformed covid related deaths across nearly 200 countries. By April 28, 2024 there have been 775 million confirmed cases globally.

Chapter 10

Human Death and Immortality

The idea of human immortality has captivated the mankind for millennia, showing up mythology, religion, and science fiction. It is just like the apprehension of our mind before the testing of nuclear bomb or more than that. While living for ever from now may have appealing effect but the consequences is perhaps more horrible than imagined. We are going to discuss some of the pros and cons of immortality in science view keeping separate philosophical, religious, spiritual outcome of such immortality.

Challenges are many

- **The idea of human immortality** may have come up to someone's mind like the creation of nuclear bomb. Nature is abundant with panorama of natural creation. Immortality is bestowed to other organism but not to Human. Turritopsis dohrnii or known as immortal jellyfish is biologically immortal. After becoming a sexually mature adult, it can transform itself back in to polyp using the cell conversion method of trans differentiation. Turritopsis dohrnii repeats this cycle means it has indefinite life span. Its immortal adaptation has allowed it to spread from its original habitat in Caribbean sea to all over the world. Biologists use the term 'immortal' to describe the cells that are not subject to Hayflick Limit. The Hayflick limit refers to the point at which the cells no longer divide due to DNA damage, or shortened telomeres. In case of Turritopsis dohrnii ther is no thermodynamic necessity for senescence: a defining feature of life is that it takes in the free energy from the environment and unloads its entropy as waste. These theories does not apply to more complex human body structures.

- **Earth's Future**: First thing the first near impossibility regarding the immortality is that, we are talking the matter in this earth's context. Beyond our planet the existence of life (alien) is unknown. Earth's Future itself will be challenging, as it has limited life span. In about 2 billion years the sun's luminosity will increase causing ocean to evaporate. Roughly 1.3 billion years of now the human may not physiologically survive due to extreme of heat and humidity. Therefore scientist are opting out various methods for immortality.

  Even if we succeed in our efforts other issues are enormous and more disastrous.

- **Population overgrowth**- Death history as discussed earlier proves the eternal truth 'once born on this earth is destined to die.' Leave aside for now the topic of soul or consciousness association with physical body. From now if by any act, human become immortal and other factors like growth, development, and reproduction continues and diseases are eliminated, then the earth will be burdened with overpopulation, putting immense pressure on resources, like food safe drinking water, and energy. However such impact on natural resources, again, as argued, depends upon the life extension and true immortality. Moderate life extension like people living up to 120 years will have little effect, but Radical life extension like life expectancy up to 1000 will have drastic effect as projected from studies. It is seen that each additional year contributes to the carbon foot print, ecological foot print, and overall resource consumption. Longer life could exacerbate habitat destruction, deforestation, and overfishing putting additional strain on natural Ecosystem. Dutch public health foresight report suggest that if mortality is reduced by 50% by 2040, the population will be larger than expected. It will affect the housing, work and retirement.

- **Social n Ethical implication**. Conflict will be intense, between the immortal group and mortal group. also augment inter group conflict. The aspiration for eternal life might lead to competition over limited resources or power struggle. Personal ego of two separate group will have effect on marriages and family life. The society will be divided in the line of HAVE and HAVENOTS.

- **Ethical Dilemmas**. Personal choices related to immortality would involve risks and trade-offs. Deciding between rejuvenation, brain uploading and other technology would be Ethically complex.

- **Values and relationship**. Mortality has shaped our values, relationship, and understanding of the world. Immortals will have no experiences of birth and death. Two groups will be divided on this line

- **Existential crisis and psychological challenges**. Immortality will lead to existential boredom due to repetition and exhaustion of life experiences. Moreover if our brain cells can memorise and corelate and have healthy out put of all years of experiences, then there will be immense psychological imbalance.

To Find A Way Out Are

Voyager Probes; The voyager1 and voyager2 spacecraft have made journey, to outer space, currently 15 billion miles away from earth carry golden records (Jimmy Carter's message) with message from humanity. These records could last for trillions of years without coming close to any stars They serve as tangible legacy to be discovered by any alien civilisation in future.

Technological immortality: Some scientist and futurists speculate about technological immortality by mind uploading. It is still a hypothetical process of transferring a person's consciousness, thoughts, memories, and personality from their biological brain to a digital substrate (such as a computer, robot, or cyberspace.)

Biological immortality: Details of the researches to reverse or to halt the aging process are beyond preview of the discussion here. But some worth mentioning are

Young Blood Rejuvenation.

Ripamycin and cellular signalling.

Cellular Reprogramming.

DNA Repair and Transposable Elements.

Telomeres and Senescence.

There exist still optimism in spite of all odd arguments on immortality. In this regard the futurologist's opinions are remarkable.

Ray Kurzweil, a renowned, inventor, computer scientist, author of books on transhumanism, health technology, and futurism. He was born on 12th February 1948 in Queens, NEW YORK CITY.

He believes that human will be able to achieve immortality or at least super- long -term longevity with in about 40 years of now. He predicts that advancement of biotechnology, Nanotechnology, and Artificial Intelligence will be able to transcend the natural limitations. Dr Ian Pearson was a British labour party politician, an MP, from 1994 until 2010, envision the immortality issue. He predicts that human will be immortal by 2050.

The changing perspective is seen in term of more positive outcome and shift is toward science and technology from religious and mythology.

Some of the positive outcome can be enumerated here

1. Immortality offers an opportunity to enjoy **infinite life span** eliminating the fear of death.

2. It may allow **extended time period** for expanded knowledge, learning, self improvement, acquiring multiple skills. Advance scientific programme may provide the ground for research and technological progress.

3. May prevent the humane from **Extinct**.

4. There will be opportunity to **explore universe**.

5. Witnessing the **historical events** and keeping records for future reference.

6. Eradication of **age related diseases**.

Chapter 11

Conclusion

At the end I think we have moved round the clock of time in defining ourself as to 'WHO AM I' in scientific perspective, the very purpose of this book. We the human are most advanced, intelligent and very optimistic in nature. We live in hopes not in despair, even if knowing that future is always uncertain.

We must admit the majesty of unknown. The universe is vast and unexplored to large extent. Humane life is a tiny dot and complex, not explained to fullest extent in this oceans of creations. Quest to define the life itself is a wonderful scientific and spiritual journey (to my belief the society can not be devoid of spiritual belief and religion.). Exploring and defining any life form out side our mother earth will help us broadening our concept of life. Finding out an exoplanet for human habitation is challenging though, may be a possibility in future.

Science has made incredible advancement in knowledge of human biology from simple atom to complex molecules to self replicating systems. Synthetic biology which combines engineering principle with biotechnology techniques to build biological organism can be hope of understanding the mechanism of body functioning. Human have the unique property of consciousness.

This the most unanswered principle existing in the physical system of human.

Life on earth is a complex interdependent web. The air we inhale, the food we intake, the earth on which we build our homes are all gift of nature. The bird who sings on the branch of a tree, the roaring tiger in deep forest, the dolphin who even sing a song for us, all these ecosystem enrich our life and bare need of life as well. Earth is the only home that we have for us and for future generations. We must live a life full of joy and happiness. To fulfil that objective we must act sensibly. STEWARDSHIP MUST COME FROM WITH IN US.